THE PATH
TO EQUALITY

THE PATH TO EQUALITY

FROM THE SCOTTSBORO CASE TO THE BREAKING OF BASEBALL'S COLOR BARRIER (1931–1947)

Darlene Clark Hine

CHELSEA HOUSE PUBLISHERS
New York   Philadelphia

FRONTISPIECE Marian Anderson sings in front of the Lincoln Memorial in Washington, D.C. The 1939 concert, staged at the historic site after the Daughters of the American Revolution refused to let Anderson use their hall, attracted a record crowd of 75,000 Americans of all races.

ON THE COVER Slugger Jackie Robinson, the first African American to play big-league baseball, crosses home plate after blasting a three-run homer for the Montreal Royals in 1946.

Chelsea House Publishers
Editorial Director Richard Rennert
Executive Managing Editor Karyn Gullen Browne
Copy Chief Robin James
Picture Editor Adrian G. Allen
Creative Director Robert Mitchell
Art Director Joan Ferrigno
Production Manager Sallye Scott

Milestones in Black American History
Senior Editor Marian W. Taylor
Series Originator and Adviser Benjamin I. Cohen
Series Consultants Clayborne Carson, Darlene Clark Hine

Staff for THE PATH TO EQUALITY
Assistant Editor Mary Sisson
Designer Cambraia Magalhães
Picture Researcher Pat Burns

First Printing

1 3 5 7 9 8 6 4 2

Library of Congress Cataloging-in-Publication Data

Hine, Darlene Clark.
   The path to equality: from the Scottsboro case to the breaking of baseball's color barrier, 1931–1947 / Darlene Clark Hine.
      p. cm. — (Milestones in Black American history)
   Includes bibliographical references and index.
      ISBN 0-7910-2251-X
      ISBN 0-7910-2677-9 (pbk.)
1. Afro-Americans—History—1877–1964—Juvenile literature. [1. Afro-Americans—History—1877–1964.] I. Title. II. Series.
E185.61.H65 1995
973.0496073—dc20
                                                              93-16016
                                                              CIP
                                                              AC

CONTENTS

	Introduction	7
	Milestones: 1931-1947	9
1	Scottsboro	15
2	Racial Politics in the 1930s	33
3	New Frontiers: Colleges, Courts, and Ballot Boxes	49
4	From Bojangles to Bigger: The Rise of Black Popular Culture	63
5	Organizations and Attitudes	83
6	The Home Front	97
7	Service to One's Country	111
8	After the War	131
	Further Reading	148
	Index	149

MILESTONES IN BLACK AMERICAN HISTORY

ANCIENT EGYPT, ETHIOPIA, AND NUBIA

THE WEST AFRICAN KINGDOMS (750–1900)

THE AGE OF DISCOVERY AND THE SLAVE TRADE

FROM THE ARRIVAL OF THE ENSLAVED AFRICANS
TO THE END OF THE AMERICAN REVOLUTION (1619–1784)

FROM THE FRAMING OF THE CONSTITUTION
TO *WALKER'S APPEAL* (1787–1829)

FROM THE NAT TURNER REVOLT
TO THE FUGITIVE SLAVE LAW (1831–1850)

FROM *UNCLE TOM'S CABIN*
TO THE ONSET OF THE CIVIL WAR (1851–1861)

FROM THE EMANCIPATION PROCLAMATION
TO THE CIVIL RIGHTS BILL OF 1875 (1863–1875)

FROM THE END OF RECONSTRUCTION
TO THE ATLANTA COMPROMISE (1877–1895)

FROM THE "SEPARATE BUT EQUAL" DOCTRINE
TO THE BIRTH OF THE NAACP (1896–1909)

FROM THE GREAT MIGRATION
TO THE HARLEM RENAISSANCE (1910–1930)

FROM THE SCOTTSBORO CASE
TO THE BREAKING OF BASEBALL'S COLOR BARRIER (1931–1947)

FROM THE DESEGREGATION OF THE ARMED FORCES
TO THE MONTGOMERY BUS BOYCOTT (1948–1956)

FROM THE FOUNDING OF THE SOUTHERN CHRISTIAN
LEADERSHIP CONFERENCE TO THE
ASSASSINATION OF MALCOLM X (1957–1965)

FROM THE SELMA– MONTGOMERY MARCH
TO THE FORMATION OF PUSH (1965–1971)

FROM THE GARY CONVENTION
TO THE PRESENT (1972–)

INTRODUCTION

In the history of black America, the dates 1931–1947 span a period of gripping drama. These were years crowded with tragedy and triumph, fear and hope, setbacks, progress, and monumental change. Perhaps not since 1865, when America's blacks at last shed slavery's bonds, had the destiny of a people so radically altered course in so short a time.

The period started ominously. Already at the bottom of the economic heap, many blacks found themselves virtually crushed by the Great Depression, the economic catastrophe that hit the nation in the 1930s. That decade also witnessed a horrifying rise in lynchings and other racially triggered violence, especially in the South. In 1929, mobs lynched 8 blacks; in the following year, 24; in 1935, 25. "Intense anti-Negro feeling has the states of the cotton belt in its grip," observed *Outlook* magazine in 1930, "and every few days it strikes down a victim." Recalling the 1930s, Walter White, longtime chief of the National Association for the Advancement of Colored People (NAACP) said, "The grim years were upon us, and interracial tensions began to mount too."

The Great Depression and its accompanying mob violence slammed into an already battered community. The U.S. Constitution's Thirteenth Amendment (ratified in 1865) freed black Americans from slavery but not from oppression; although legally recognized as citizens, blacks still faced an ongoing battle against intolerance and injustice.

In the mid-1930s, 70 years after the last Civil War gun fell silent, few blacks had experienced the true splendors of "America the Beautiful." Schoolchildren might sing of "brotherhood from sea to shining sea," but blacks received inferior educations, lower pay for similar work, and limited chances to advance. Segregated in every area of life, continually exposed to racial harassment, and often denied the protection and equality mandated by the Constitution, most blacks found the American Dream an unattainable myth.

But as the 1930s rolled into the 1940s, a series of events—some small and now largely forgotten, some major and historically significant—began to suggest the possibility of change, of hope. These were years of increasing self-determination in the black community: African Americans realized that if they wanted their economic, social, cultural, and legal conditions to improve, they would have to do the improving themselves.

Armed with this knowledge, they carried the battle forward, working toward job security, the overturn of racist laws, and the destruction of racial segregation. They wanted justice before the courts, equal treatment in the armed forces, and full acceptance into every profession from nursing to big-league baseball. A period that opened with one of American history's most flagrant judicial miscarriages—the Scottsboro case—would close with blacks firmly entrenched in many once restricted fields—including one in Brooklyn, New York, called Ebbets.

MILESTONES
1931–1947

1930 • Jesse Binga, founder and president of Chicago's first black-owned-and-operated bank, refuses to seize the assets of his depression-struck black customers. As a result, he loses the bank and goes to prison; he receives a presidential pardon in 1933 but never recovers his bank or his fortune.

1931 • After a blatantly unfair trial that stirs international outrage, nine black youths are convicted of raping two white women in Scottsboro, Alabama. A decade later the innocent "Scottsboro boys" are finally cleared; by then they have served a total of 75 years in prison.

• Walter White begins 24 years of service as chief of the National Association for the Advancement of Colored People (NAACP). Under his leadership, NAACP membership increases from 70,000 to 250,000 people.

1932 • Democrat Franklin Delano Roosevelt is elected president of the United States.

• Performing with clarinetist Benny Goodman, jazz singer Billie Holiday makes her first recording.

1934 • NAACP lawyer Thurgood Marshall organizes a boycott in Baltimore, Maryland, steering shoppers away from white-owned stores that are patronized by blacks but that refuse to hire black workers. The shopkeepers sue the NAACP, but Marshall's inspired defense produces a surprise victory. (Thirty-three years later, Marshall will become the first African American to serve on the U.S. Supreme Court.)

1935 • Residents of Harlem, New York, hear that a white policeman has killed a young black robbery suspect. The rumor is false, but pent-up anger at economic and racial injustice explodes in a night of rioting that costs three lives and millions of dollars in destroyed property.

- Mary McLeod Bethune, founder of Florida's Bethune-Cookman College, wins the NAACP's coveted Spingarn Medal and founds the National Council of Negro Women.

- After the University of Maryland tells qualified black student Donald Murray that it "does not accept Negro students," NAACP lawyers Charles Houston and Thurgood Marshall go to work, eventually earning a stunning triumph in the U.S. Supreme Court case *Murray v. Pearson*.

- Congress forces the Pullman Company, owner and operator of much of the nation's railroad equipment, to meet with the Brotherhood of Sleeping Car Porters, a black labor union organized by activist A. Philip Randolph.

1936

- Roosevelt appoints Mary McLeod Bethune administrative assistant for Negro affairs of the National Youth Administration (NYA), a federal youth employment agency. Impressed by her NYA work, the president later puts Bethune in charge of the new Division of Negro Affairs; the 61-year-old educator thereby becomes America's first black female to head a federal agency.

1937

- William Henry Hastie becomes the first black federal judge when he is appointed to the U.S. District Court for the U.S. Virgin Islands.

- Boxer Joe Louis (often called the Brown Bomber) becomes world heavyweight champion by knocking out James J. Braddock in the eighth round of the championship match.

1938

- The U.S. Supreme Court hears the case of Lloyd Gaines, a black college graduate rejected by the University of Missouri Law School on racial grounds. Representing Gaines, the NAACP's Marshall-Houston team convinces the Court that Missouri's proposal—to comply with the "separate-but-equal" doctrine by paying Gaines's tuition in an out-of-state school—is unconstitutional. From this point on, each state must integrate its graduate schools or build brand-new schools for blacks.

- The U.S. Army decrees that the number of black recruits cannot exceed the proportion (10 percent) of blacks in the general population.

1939

- Nazi Germany invades Poland; Britain and France declare war against Germany. World War II has begun.

- Celebrated concert singer Marian Anderson is barred from Constitution Hall, a Washington, D.C., auditorium owned by the all-white Daughters of the American Revolution (DAR). Aided by First Lady Eleanor Roosevelt, the NAACP's Walter White, and other activists, Anderson gives a free Easter Sunday concert at the Lincoln Memorial, an unprecedented event drawing 75,000 Americans of every race.

- NAACP chief Walter White creates the Legal Defense and Education Fund (always known simply as "the Fund"), a branch of the organization that will provide free legal aid to black victims of racial injustice. Thurgood Marshall is appointed director-council of the Fund.

- Hattie McDaniel wins an Academy Award for her performance as Mammy in *Gone with the Wind,* thereby becoming the first African American so honored. Criticized by some for playing a stereotypical happy servant, McDaniel and other black actors form the Fair Play Committee, aimed at persuading the movie industry to offer blacks better roles and to cleanse films of racist language.

1940

- Richard Wright publishes *Native Son,* a best-selling novel about the effects of racial oppression in America. Finally overwhelmed by his nation's prejudice, the prize-winning author will move to France permanently in 1947.

- Blood-research pioneer Charles Drew becomes head of the Blood for Britain project. The program uses Drew's own technique for stockpiling blood supplies, drying and storing plasma instead of whole blood.

- Congress passes the Selective Training and Service Act of 1940, a peacetime-draft law aimed at ensuring adequate troop levels in the event of a war. The act prohibits discriminatory induction practices but does not bar segregation or discrimination within the services.

- Colonel Benjamin O. Davis, Sr., is promoted to brigadier general, making him the highest-ranking black officer in the U.S. armed services.

1941

- President Roosevelt issues Executive Order 8802, which prohibits racial discrimination in the defense industry and establishes the Fair Employment Practices Committee (FEPC). The order is the direct result of pressure applied by Walter White and A. Philip Randolph; the two black leaders had threatened to stage a Washington, D.C., protest march of 100,000 African Americans if the president failed to act against employment discrimination.

- December 7: Japan bombs the U.S. naval base at Pearl Harbor, Hawaii, bringing the United States into World War II.

- Dorie Miller, a 22-year-old black messman in the U.S. Navy, braves the hail of Japanese bombs at Pearl Harbor to carry his wounded commander to safety on the battleship *Arizona*. Although untrained in artillery, Miller then mans the machine gun of a fallen mate and shoots down as many as six enemy aircraft before running out of ammunition. The young messman later receives a Navy Cross for heroism; six months later, he goes down with his ship in a Pacific naval battle.

- The U.S. Army Air Corps's all-black unit, the 99th Pursuit Squadron, proves itself a roaring success, thus putting to rest all doubts about blacks' courage or willingness to fight.

- The Army Nurse Corps grudgingly accepts 56 black volunteers.

1942

- The Women's Army Auxiliary Corps (WAC) is created to train women for service tasks, thereby freeing male soldiers for combat. Although the WAC maintains a 10 percent racial quota on enlistments and demands racial segregation on bases, it does allow black women to command white recruits, and it permits blacks to enter technical schools and officers' training schools.

1943

- Race riots break out in Detroit, Michigan. Finally quelled by federal troops, the violence leaves 34 people dead and more than $2 million in property damage. One month later, in August, New York City's Harlem experiences similar rioting, but quick police action keeps the death toll to six people.

- The American Bar Association admits its first black member.

- The army raises its quota of African American nurses to 160.

- The DAR invites Marian Anderson to perform in its Constitution Hall, the auditorium from which it had barred her four years earlier.

1944

- The FEPC forces the city of Philadelphia, Pennsylvania, to promote eight African Americans to the position of streetcar drivers. White drivers protest with a five-day strike, but the federal government stands firm, breaking the strike with troops. Eager to prevent future problems, Philadelphia opens more city jobs to blacks.

- During the six-week-long Battle of the Bulge, a massive German assault on Allied lines in Belgium, U.S. Army officials offer black soldiers the opportunity to "share the glory of victory" with the beleaguered white troops on the front line. Thousands of black soldiers rush to the battle, where they earn the respect of their white comrades by demonstrating superb fighting abilities.

- Tackling the so-called white primary—a process by which southern blacks were effectively disfranchised—Thurgood Marshall argues the case of *Smith v. Allwright* before the Supreme Court. The NAACP lawyer scores a decisive victory, sealing the right of all races to join political parties.

1945
- The U.S. Marine Corps commissions its first African American officer.
- The army agrees to accept nurses without regard to race and is quickly flooded with African American volunteers. The navy soon follows suit, announcing a nondiscriminatory policy toward black nurses.

1946
- The navy removes all restrictions on black personnel and prohibits racial segregation in naval housing and facilities.
- In the first of his many acts to promote racial equality, Congressman Adam Clayton Powell, Jr., moves to prevent federal school-lunch programs from excluding black children. Loathed by his southern colleagues but wildly popular with his Harlem constituents, Powell will be returned to Congress 13 times.
- Spurred on by Walter White and other black activists, President Harry S. Truman, Roosevelt's successor, sets up the Committee on Civil Rights. The group is empowered to investigate civil-liberties violations and recommend steps to correct them.

1947
- Slugger Jackie Robinson makes sports—and American—history when he signs on with the Brooklyn Dodgers, becoming the major leagues' first African American player. Robinson's breakthrough is soon followed by Roy Campanella and other black players.

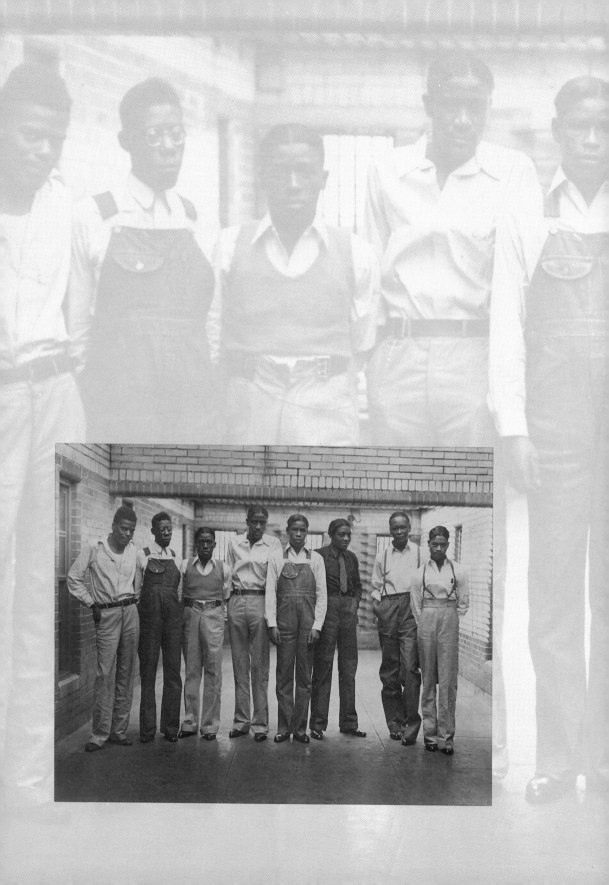

1

SCOTTSBORO

On October 29, 1929, the U.S. stock market crashed. A decade of wild, uncontrolled borrowing and lending had so weakened the market that stock prices tumbled, rapidly destroying the "paper wealth" on which many of the nation's largest businesses operated. Public confidence plummeted along with stock prices, resulting in an avalanche of business closings, bank failures, mine and mill shutdowns, farm abandonments, and a calamitously sudden job shortage.

In less than two years, production of goods and services dropped almost 30 percent, and unemployment rose from 1.5 million to 12.1 million. By the mid-1930s, one in every four white workers had lost his or her job; for blacks, the figure was one in every two. From 1929 to 1940, the Great Depression had America by the throat; in the case of blacks, it was a stranglehold. Growing numbers of families could no longer afford adequate food and clothing. Many Americans became discouraged, doubting that condi-

Eight of the nine Scottsboro defendants line up for a portrait in Birmingham, Alabama. The case of the "Scottsboro boys," as the nine young men wrongly convicted of rape were called, commanded international attention in the 1930s and 1940s.

15

tions would ever improve or that they would ever again enjoy good times. Everybody suffered, but African Americans were hardest hit of all. It was a time defined by what one observer called "a bitter bit of poetry: 'The Negro, Last Hired and First Fired.' "

The depression struck America after a remarkable period of black migration. During America's involvement in World War I (1917–18), large numbers of rural southern blacks had departed their homes for the cities, in a quest for work. Some went voluntarily; others had been forced off the land by the white merchants, bankers, and landowners to whom they owed money. By the early 1930s, close to two million of these migrants traveled America.

When the stock market crashed in 1929, large numbers of transplanted southern blacks had found household or personal-service jobs; these were among the first work categories wiped out by the depression. Blacks employed in factories also lost their jobs quickly; those who worked on farms found themselves either dismissed or working for starvation-level wages. Because few of these generally ill-paid blacks had saved much money, they began to suffer almost immediately.

By 1934, the government classed 17 percent of white citizens as no longer capable of self-support. For blacks, the figure stood at 38 percent overall, with even more appalling numbers in southern cities. In Atlanta, Georgia, 65 percent of black workers were in need of public assistance, and in Norfolk, Virginia, a stunning 80 percent were forced to apply for welfare.

Although many blacks were so badly off before the depression that they barely noticed its arrival, others had begun to make real economic progress. From these hardworking people, the depression snatched savings, farms, homes, and businesses. Emerging black companies had been a source of heightened pride and self-esteem for the black community, to which they had

begun to provide important job opportunities. The massive destruction of these businesses dealt a shocking blow to blacks of all classes.

Among the depression's major casualties was the Binga State Bank, Chicago's first black-owned-and-operated financial institution. The bank had been founded in 1908 by Jesse Binga (1865–1950), a Detroit-born real estate broker who served as its president. Astonishing most of the white-controlled banking world, Binga managed his bank so successfully that by 1930, its deposits had grown to $1.5 million—a remarkable figure for a private bank in that era.

The depression—along with Binga's sense of brotherhood—proved his undoing. He had invested

Puzzled and worried, depositors mill around the locked and guarded doors of a bank in Hamtramck, Michigan, in 1932. More than 10,000 banks failed during the Great Depression, wiping out the life savings of millions of Americans.

much of the bank's assets in mortgage loans to blacks. When the borrowers lost their jobs, they were unable to meet their payments, but Binga refused to foreclose (seize the debtors' homes and farms). As a result, on July 30, 1930, state bank auditors padlocked the big, once flourishing institution on Chicago's South Side, an action that brought Binga to court on a federal misuse-of-funds charge. Sentenced to prison in 1932, Binga was pardoned by Democratic president Franklin D. Roosevelt a year later, but he was never able to rebuild his bank or his fortune. Still, his career encouraged young blacks aspiring to enter the once all-white world of business and finance.

But in 1930, *aspiring* was an almost forgotten word; the economy was locked into a deep freeze. A month after officials sealed Binga's bank, the black newspaper *Chicago Defender* ran a chilling bit of advice, headlined GET FIXED:

> Times are not what they used to be. There is no use shutting our eyes to this fact. Prosperity has gone into retirement. . . . Our advice is for everyone to get something, and hold onto it. Get it in the city if possible, but, failing this, start toward the farm before the snow flies.

And indeed, across America, thousands of blacks were starting to move, but most of them away from rather than toward the farm. Hunting for work, many African American men changed location repeatedly. Some migrated to southern cities; finding no jobs there, they hopped freight trains or hitched rides to northern cities—Chicago, Detroit, Pittsburgh, New York—hoping to land work in factories, steel mills, or meatpacking houses.

Few succeeded. During the depression, even the backbreaking jobs—low-status, low-paying labor that white workers had once dismissed as "Negro work" beneath their dignity—were eagerly sought by those same whites. And it went without saying that when given a choice, white supervisors hired white workers.

Author Thomas Wolfe wrote of the army of displaced men searching for work:

These were the wanderers from town to town, the riders of freight trains, the thumbers of rides on highways, the uprooted, unwanted male population of America. They drifted across the land and gathered in the big cities when winter came, hungry, defeated, empty, hopeless, restless, driven by they knew not what, always on the move, looking everywhere for work, for the bare crumbs to support their miserable lives, and finding neither work nor crumbs.

Black women, too, left the rural South to search for work. In the urban North, they found themselves discriminated against not only because of race but

Tense but unflinching, young black Floridians face a band of Ku Klux Klan "knights" in 1938. As the Great Depression deepened, economic competition between blacks and whites increased and racial tensions worsened.

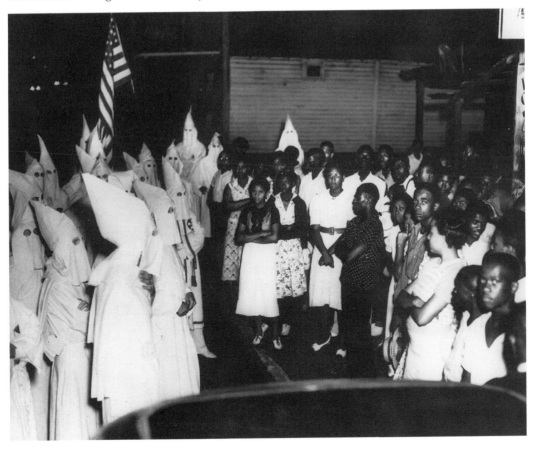

because of gender; office and factory jobs were totally beyond their reach. The rare southern black woman who did find employment worked as a household domestic or laundress, occupations at the bottom of the labor scale. A black housemaid who worked 10 hours per day for six and one-half days might expect to earn $5.

To make the problems of black employment-seekers infinitely worse, few labor unions accepted black members. Most local unions affiliated with the national American Federation of Labor barred blacks or limited them to segregated locals, and the railroad unions, ironically known as "brotherhoods," excluded blacks entirely. With jobs scarce and people increasingly nervous and fearful, racial hatreds grew worse than ever, not least on the labor front. In 1932, for example, when the Illinois Central Railroad hired a group of black firemen, white rail workers reacted with fury. Within a few months, the whites had ambushed and killed seven of the black firemen and seriously injured another eight. No arrests were made in the case.

Most African Americans believed it futile to look to President Herbert Hoover's Republican administration for relief. As Walter White put it, Hoover "sat stolidly in the White House, refusing bluntly to receive Negro citizens who wished to lay before him the facts of their steadily worsening plight or to consider any remedial legislation or governmental action. His attitude toward Negroes caused me to coin a phrase which gained considerable currency, particularly in the Negro world, in which I described Hoover as 'the man in the lily-White House.'"

Walter White, born in Georgia in 1893, served as director of the National Association for the Advancement of Colored People (NAACP) from 1931 to 1955. One of America's greatest

but least recognized heroes in the long battle for civil rights, the blond-haired, fair-skinned, blue-eyed African American could easily have passed for white but never even considered it. Instead, this quiet but forceful man spent most of his life crusading for racial justice, improved black schools, and an end to discrimination, segregation, and racial violence, especially lynching. Personally investigating 42 lynchings and 8 race riots, White repeatedly risked his life for the cause he believed in. Under his leadership, the NAACP grew from a relatively weak association with 70,000 members to a powerful force for black rights, a quarter of a million strong.

Walter White, long-term chief of the National Association for the Advancement of Colored People (NAACP), was commonly mistaken for a white man, but he never considered passing for one. Quiet but fiercely courageous, the Georgia-born activist dedicated his life to seeking justice for his race.

President Hoover insisted that business conditions would get better by themselves. He refused to permit the use of federal funds to aid the unemployed, maintaining that relief was the concern of local governments and private charities. Everything would soon be back to "normal," said Hoover, and in the meantime, no Americans were starving. But Hoover was wrong. People all over the nation, with blacks in the majority, were suffering terribly.

As historian Milton Meltzer points out in *The Black Americans* (Harper, 1984), "The welfare figures showed they starved in the mountains of Kentucky and on the plains of Kansas. They starved in the cities and the villages. And they died. Thousands of children died of the Depression disease—not enough to eat."

As more people lost their jobs and their homes, increasing numbers of men, women, and children began wandering the streets or settling into what they called, with grim humor, "Hoovervilles." Springing up around railroad tracks and dumps, Hoovervilles were clusters of shacks made of tin, cardboard, and burlap. Although many people, both black and white, despaired at such conditions, others would never knuckle under to misery. These tough-minded activists, among them numerous African Americans, insisted that conditions could improve and must improve, and they started working toward that improvement.

Staring into the bleak face of the Great Depression, many black women and men refused to flinch. Instead, they began to seize the initiative, trying to help themselves and their communities. Mutual aid societies, churches, women's clubs, civil rights organizations, and religious groups opened up soup kitchens, collected and dispersed clothing, and provided shelter and even health care for the most needy. For many African Americans, this reliance on self-help and racial solidarity launched a new era of black resistance and militancy.

One avenue toward self-help involved black churches. In New York City's Harlem, where about half of the 200,000 residents depended on unemployment relief, the Abyssinian Baptist Church established its own relief operation, staffed by local citizens. In the first three months of 1931, the Abyssinian Baptist Relief Bureau served 28,500 free meals, and distributed 525 food baskets, 17,928 pieces of clothing, and 2,564 pairs of shoes.

Another homegrown dispenser of aid to the poor was Father Divine, a celebrated black evangelist who settled in Harlem in 1915. Blending his own form of religion (Divine proclaimed that he himself was "the living God") with moral lectures ("Stop committing vice and crime and sin and debauchery of any kind," he preached), Divine attracted thousands of followers, most (but not all) of them black. All during the depression, the Father Divine Peace Mission provided jobs, shelter, and food to Harlem's poor. His operation, a religious cooperative, followed the pattern of black self-help: participants received what they needed and gave what income and labor they could afford. Divine mysteriously produced daily free feasts for the hungry, urging them to show their appreciation only by returning service to the community.

Other Harlemites helped each other in their own ways: black nightclub owners staged special events, donating the admission money to the needy; black actors and singers performed at fund-raising benefits; black friends and neighbors gave "rent parties" to prevent families from being evicted from their apart-

Evangelist Father Divine receives a platter of chicken from his wife, Mother Divine, during a 1937 banquet. Father Divine, who claimed to be "the living God," opened a Harlem mission that provided jobs, shelter, and food to the poor throughout the depression.

ments for nonpayment; black housewives formed food cooperatives, buying supplies in large quantities to obtain the lowest possible prices.

In another form of taking charge of their lives, black citizens began to demand that the businesses they patronized employ black workers. In 1932, for example, black customers in Cleveland, Ohio, requested that local dairy companies hire black milkmen. When the dairies refused, a group of black businessmen formed a dairy organization of their own. The new operation provided employment opportunities for black drivers, office personnel, and milkmen.

Cleveland's was simply part of a nationwide black crusade to increase the economic viability of black communities. African Americans in Chicago, New York, Detroit, and dozens of other cities used direct-action tactics, starting with hard-hitting "Don't buy where you can't work" campaigns. They marched, picketed, and boycotted white-owned businesses in black neighborhoods, trying to force them to provide blacks a fair share of clerical and management positions.

The "Don't buy where you can't work" technique proved effective. In Chicago, for example, a black boycott persuaded the giant Woolworth chain of variety stores to hire, for the first time in its history, black clerks at its South Side outlets. And in Harlem, the Negro Industrial and Clerical League picketed tirelessly, forcing dozens of white shopkeepers to start employing local citizens.

In 1934, a young NAACP lawyer in Baltimore, Maryland, decided to protest the refusal of local white merchants to hire black workers, even in shops that depended on black customers. Organizing a group of unemployed black high school graduates into a picket line, the lawyer succeeded in keeping black shoppers away from the stores, and sales plummeted. When outraged merchants sued the NAACP, the young lawyer volunteered to defend it. To everyone's surprise, including the lawyer's, the white federal judge not only ruled in the NAACP's favor but congratulated the lawyer—an up-and-coming civil rights fighter named Thurgood Marshall.

Another powerful consumer group, the Greater New York Coordinating Committee, was led by the Reverend Adam Clayton Powell, Jr., pastor of Harlem's Abyssinian Baptist Church. Powell later described the committee's methods:

> We set out to blitzkrieg 125th Street. We made it a disgrace for any Negro to cross a picket line.... We picked the largest . . . stores and picketed them simultaneously. Black phalanxes marched in front with signs crying— "Don't buy where you can't work." . . . The Street, as 125th is called, was in a turmoil. We didn't look like a group of Negroes that could be split; nor did we seem to be the kind whose indignation would pass away overnight. The exploiters began to bargain. Some attempted to buy us out, but Uncle Tom was dead.

Detroit, Michigan, gave birth to one of the nation's most successful self-help economic movements. In 1930 a group of 50 black women formed the Housewives' League of Detroit. The organization's only membership requirement was a pledge to support black businesses, buy black products, and patronize black professionals, thereby keeping blacks' money in the black community.

The Housewives' League relied on "directed spending" campaigns. Groups of women would visit neighborhood merchants and businesses and ask them to hire local youths or to carry black-produced products. If the managers refused, the women would no longer purchase goods and services from them. By 1934, the Detroit league's rolls had expanded from the original 50 to 10,000 members. Spurred by a combination of economic nationalism and black women's self-determination, the league quickly spread to Chicago, Baltimore, Washington, New York, Cleveland,

In 1937, Thurgood Marshall, an eloquent and brilliant young NAACP lawyer, organized a successful black student boycott against Baltimore stores that refused to hire blacks. When the stores sued the NAACP, Marshall represented the organization— and won.

The Reverend Adam Clayton Powell, Jr., pastor of Harlem's Abyssinian Baptist Church, delivers a rousing sermon in 1937. A highly effective political crusader, Powell organized a number of antidiscrimination demonstrations, and soon became well known as a militant advocate of racial equality.

and many other cities. Such organized efforts created new jobs for blacks and helped prevent total economic collapse in the black community.

In hard times, many people look for a scapegoat—something or someone to blame for their troubles—and in the depression, competition for jobs and affordable housing made racial hostility worse than ever. Blacks in northern cities faced not only unemployment and hunger but sudden, uncontrollable violence, and both races regularly confronted each other in bloody street fights. The bitter and destructive Harlem Riot of 1935, however, grew from roots even more tangled than interracial anger.

Pulling together, Harlem citizens had made great strides in improving life in their community. Nevertheless, the depression created problems that sometimes seemed insurmountable. Thousands of new residents had strained Harlem's resources to the breaking point; it was not uncommon to find four families sharing one dilapidated single-room apartment. If the living quarters were bad, the rents were worse. Not all Harlem's apartment buildings were white-owned, but many were, along with a majority of the community's shops.

When a false rumor—that white policemen had killed a black Harlem youth accused of stealing from a local store—hit the streets on March 19, 1935, it triggered instant rioting. Furious about the supposed fate of the boy (whom the police had actually only questioned briefly, then sent home), and deeply, permanently angry about the insults, abuses, and hardships they suffered as "second-class citizens," Harlem's residents suddenly exploded. At the close of a night of smashing and looting, three blacks were dead; scores of people, black and white, lay injured; 200 stores were in ruins; and millions of dollars worth of damage had been done.

Harlem's 1935 night of violence has sometimes

been described as a race riot, but this is inaccurate.
Black writer Claude McKay, an eyewitness, put it this
way: "There was no manifest hostility between colored or white as such. . . . White persons, singly and
in groups, walked the streets of Harlem without being
molested."

The objects of black rage that night were stores,
symbols of white control over blacks. Indeed, an investigation conducted by the city of New York concluded that the riot was caused by what investigators
termed "resentments against racial discrimination and
poverty in the midst of plenty."

Poverty pushed countless people of all races, many
of them young, all of them homeless and jobless, onto
the railroads. They traveled, of course, not in the
luxury of windowed Pullmans but on the rods beneath
the trains or in the freight cars. No one knew the
number of these stowaways, or *hoboes,* as they were
commonly called, but one railroad, the Southern Pacific, reported throwing 683,000 people off its freight
cars in one year of the Great Depression.

Male hoboes often obtained food by stealing from
produce trucks or farmhouses. Women sometimes survived by selling themselves for dimes and quarters to
their fellow wanderers, white or black. Such a life was
difficult anywhere in the country, but in the South,
where interracial sexual relations were legally forbid-
den, it was highly dangerous. Caught with a black
man, a white prostitute could face not only criminal
charges but potential public fury. To escape, she might
cry "rape"—exonerating herself but exposing her cus-
tomer to murder by a lynch mob.

Apparently this is what happened in the
Scottsboro case, which began on a freight train
nearing Scottsboro, Alabama. On the night of
March 25, 1931, a group of young white hoboes

accosted a group of young black hoboes on the slow-moving train; the blacks pitched them off. Filing a complaint with the Scottsboro sheriff, the whites said they had been viciously assaulted by black hoodlums.

"Round up every Negro on the train," the sheriff ordered his deputies. A sweep of the train netted nine young black men: Ozie Powell, Clarence Norris, Charlie Weems, Olen Montgomery, Willie Roberson, Haywood Patterson, Eugene Williams, Andy Wright, and Roy Wright. To the lawmen's surprise, their search of the train also revealed two young white women: 19-year-old Victoria Price and 17-year-old Ruby Bates.

Apparently afraid of being arrested, the women claimed they had been attacked—by the nine youths already in custody. The black boys and men (their ages ranged from 13 to 20) now stood accused of rape, at that time a capital crime (one punishable by death) in the South. The sheriff locked them up. Then, almost from out of nowhere, there materialized a mob of 10,000 jeering, screaming whites. The sheriff requested National Guard backup; he wanted to keep the crowd from hanging his prisoners before the state could do it.

The town of Scottsboro instantly filled with rumors: the accused "black brutes," it was said, were known to be a monstrous danger to white women everywhere. Twelve days after the alleged crime, the trial took place. The "Scottsboro boys," as they came to be labeled, never had a chance. Their white, court-appointed attorney—widely known as an alcoholic—came to court drunk each day. The prosecutor said to the jury, "Guilty or not, let's get rid of these niggers."

Three days after the trial began, the jurors found all nine defendants guilty. Eight received the death sentence; the ninth, 13 years old, was given life imprisonment, although seven of the jurors had voted to hang him, too.

These blacks had been accused of violating one of the South's major taboos: mixed-race sex. The charges were proved false—medical examinations of Price and Bates showed that neither had been raped—but the court's verdict demonstrated that it did not matter. The defendants were black, their accusers white.

Eager to recruit more black members, the Ameri-

Washington, D.C., police break up a 1932 rally protesting the continuing imprisonment of the Scottsboro defendants. The Scottsboro case sparked demonstrations— many of them violent—across the globe.

can Communist party seized on Scottsboro. Quickly and noisily, the party's International Labor Defense arm (ILD) rose in defense of the "boys." The case's notoriety had already begun to spread; international celebrities—among them the French Nobel Prize–winning doctor Albert Schweitzer and the American novelist Theodore Dreiser—publicly protested the black youths' innocence, and all over Europe, mobs stoned American consulates. In Havana, angry Cubans bombed an American bank.

So badly did the Communists want black members that, in 1932, the party fielded a black vice presidential candidate: James W. Ford, a 39-year-old Alabamian and graduate of Fisk University, who ran with U.S. Communist party chairman William Z. Foster. In the same year, the Communists offered New Yorkers a black mayoral candidate: William L. Patterson, a lawyer who had studied in the Soviet Union. Neither Ford nor Patterson won, but their nominations pleased blacks, which was all party officials had hoped for. The Communists also made well-publicized but unsuccessful efforts to unionize the South's black sharecroppers. The party did manage to attract a number of disillusioned blacks, but few maintained their interest after 1941, when the depression ended with the start of World War II.

The National Association for the Advancement of Colored People, the preeminent black protest organization, also became involved in the Scottsboro case, but the ILD proved more effective. The party unit quickly appealed the "boys' " conviction and death sentence to the United States Supreme Court, an appeal that resulted in two important decisions.

In *Powell v. Alabama* in 1932, the Supreme Court ruled that the nine Scottsboro defendants had not been given adequate legal counsel and that the trial had taken place in a hostile and volatile atmosphere. Asserting that the youths' right to due process, as set forth in the Constitution's Fourteenth Amendment, had been violated, the Supreme Court ordered Alabama to mount a new trial. The state did as instructed, but the new trial resulted in a similar verdict of guilt and death or life imprisonment. The ILD again appealed to the Supreme Court.

In its 1935 *Norris v. Alabama* decision, the Court reaffirmed the concept that all Americans have the right to a trial by a jury of their peers. The systematic exclusion of African Americans from the Scottsboro juries, said the Court, denied the nine blacks equal protection under the law, which the Fourteenth Amendment guarantees. Reversing the Scottsboro decisions as unconstitutional, the Court called for yet another trial.

The *Norris* decision affirmed the right of blacks to serve on state-court juries. But the "boys" were still not set free. The case would, in fact, drag on for years. During that time, Ruby Bates publicly admitted that the rape charge had been a hoax; white Alabamians ignored her. In 1937, Alabama dropped its charges against five of the nine black youths, and in the 1940s, the state released the remaining four. All together, nine innocent black men had served some three-quarters of a century in prison.

By 1978, most of the "boys" had disappeared from public sight. Four were known to have died; four were either dead or in hiding. The ninth, however, retired warehouseman Clarence Willie Norris, was living in Brooklyn, New York. When a reporter asked him how he felt, Norris said, "I'm just glad to be free." Life, he added, had taught him this: "To stand up for your rights, even if it kills you. That's all life consists of."

2

RACIAL POLITICS IN THE 1930s

In 1863 Republican president Abraham Lincoln signed the Emancipation Proclamation, ostensibly signaling the end of slavery in America. In 1870 the Republican-controlled Congress passed, and the states ratified, the Constitution's Fifteenth Amendment, which gave black men the vote (women of all races would have to wait another 50 years). These actions would reward the Republican party with some six decades of black political loyalty.

In the first dozen years after the Civil War—1865 to 1877, the period known as Reconstruction—southern blacks seemed on their way to full-fledged citizenship. The vanquished white South, however, had never changed its mind about people of color. Federal legislation that guaranteed rights to African Americans originated not with their former "owners" but from the so-called Radical Republicans—the extremist, fiercely antisouthern wing of the Republican party, which controlled Congress. The Republicans installed federal troops in the South to ensure black

Eleanor Roosevelt, wife of President Franklin D. Roosevelt, presents the NAACP's 1939 Spingarn Medal to contralto Marian Anderson. The black singer had won the prestigious award in part for her magnificent voice and in part for the serene courage with which she had faced bigotry.

rights, including the right to vote and run for office.

Gradually, however, the former Confederate states gained readmittance to the Union and military law ended. By 1876, only three southern states—Florida, Louisiana, and South Carolina—retained Republican administrations. The Democrats, party of the onetime slaveholders and other ultraconservative whites, returned to power, assuring the rapid slide and eventual eclipse of black equality in the South. With the Democrats in full control, the South reverted to its old philosophy, which any old-line southerner might have summed up in four ugly words: "Keep the nigger down." By 1900, black southerners had virtually disappeared from the southern political scene.

Meanwhile, Republicans in the northern and western states were busily courting the black vote.

White citizens of Fort Lauderdale, Florida, casually inspect the body of 32-year-old Rubin Stacy, lynched by a mob of 100 whites for allegedly attacking a white woman in 1935. Such terrorist crimes were regularly committed by southerners to keep black people in "their place"—at the bottom of the political, social, and economic poles.

They had little trouble; most black voters automatically supported the "party of Lincoln." They long remembered the political views of Frederick Douglass (1817–95), the former slave who became one of the nation's best-known abolitionists, writers, editors, and lecturers: "The Republican Party is the ship," Douglass had said; "all else is the sea."

By the 1930s, however, black Americans had begun to ask questions about the Republican party: what had decades of political dues paying done for them? African Americans remained at the nation's lowest socioeconomic and political level. In the Great Depression, they had been the first to lose their jobs, their possessions, and their homes, but Republican president Herbert Hoover had done nothing to aid them. White Republicans took black voters for granted, anyway; there was no need, they thought, to do them special favors.

At this point, notes historian Robert S. McElvaine (in *The Great Depression*, 1984), "the Grand Old Party [the Republicans] offered blacks little more than the grand old platitudes of Abraham Lincoln." Understandably, black Americans now started reexamining their political options. But the Democrats offered even less than the Republicans. "At the 1928 Democratic Convention in Houston, the black alternates were seated in an area separated by chicken wire from the white delegates," reports McElvaine. "Here was a perfect symbol of the racial attitudes of the party."

In the 1932 presidential election campaign, black citizens began to keep an eye on the one candidate who seemed to be addressing their situation. Franklin Delano Roosevelt of New York promised better times and delivery of what he called "the greatest good to the greatest number of our citizens." But although the confident young Democrat and his promises intrigued black voters, they found old ties hard to break. Just as they had discovered it traumatic to move north, black

Americans now found it wrenching to shift their political allegiance. In 1932, despite their attraction to Roosevelt and their growing disenchantment with the Republicans, 75 percent of black voters chose the politically doomed Herbert Hoover.

Even without black support, Roosevelt swept to victory and immediately began to rebuild the nation's crippled economy. Announcing the start of a "New Deal for the American people," he and his administration created a bewildering array of new agencies (jokingly labeled "Roosevelt's alphabet soup" by reporters). Among the soup's many ingredients were the NRA (the National Recovery Administration, whose Blue Eagle emblem became one of the era's symbols), the AAA (Agricultural Adjustment Administration), the CCC (Civilian Conservation Corps), the NYA (National Youth Administration), and the WPA (Works Progress Administration). At first, none of these agencies specifically targeted the devastated black community; some of them helped anyway, but others made a bad situation worse.

Seeking to guarantee fair pay for workers, the NRA established wage rates according to region. Almost invariably, wages in the South were set lower than those in the rest of the country, reflecting the area's lower living costs. But because most low-level southern jobs were held by black men and women, the NRA's efforts wound up severely limiting black workers' pay.

Jobs traditionally filled by blacks—farm labor and domestic work—were not protected by the Blue Eagle at all. In some cases, the NRA covered wages of jobholders of all races, but this worked out least well of all for black workers: if white employers could not hire black workers at cheaper rates than they could hire whites, they usually hired whites. Sardonic black writers soon suggested that *NRA* really stood for "Negro Run Around."

The Agricultural Adjustment Administration also created unintended grief for African Americans. Under AAA rules, the government paid landowners not to plant crops or raise livestock on their acreage. (This plan aimed at protecting farmers by limiting production, thereby stabilizing prices.) Sharecroppers (farmers, many of them black, who worked land owned by another, sharing their crops with that owner) made up the bulk of those who tilled the South. When the government paid a landowner to take land out of production, the landowner was legally required to divide the money with his "croppers." In practice, however, owners simply kept the government payments and evicted the sharecroppers, leaving them far worse off than they were before the creation of the AAA.

For black Americans, another New Deal flaw involved its self-styled "grassroots democracy." This

Evicted from their homes, black sharecroppers camp out on a road near Sikestown, Missouri, in 1939. The Roosevelt administration's New Deal programs were well intentioned, but faced with a stone wall of white southern resistance, they did little to help the South's desperately poor rural blacks.

meant allowing local officials to run federal programs—which, in the South, put the controls into white hands, with all-too-predictable results. Historian McElvaine quotes a typical Georgia official: "There will be no Negroes," he said, "driving trucks getting forty cents an hour when the good white men and white women working in the fields alongside these roads can hardly earn forty cents a day." In Georgia, monthly payments to white people on relief (a system similar to today's welfare) averaged about 70 percent more than those received by black citizens.

Most African Americans realized that Roosevelt was doing little to help them during his first term. Those with political savvy knew why: in order to pass laws that would pull the economy out of the devastating depression, Roosevelt needed Congress. Congress was dominated by the southern wing of the Democratic party. If the president made any open moves toward equalizing the lot of the nation's black citizens, the southerners would swiftly torpedo his legislative program. He said as much to NAACP chief Walter White, who had urged him to make lynching a federal (instead of state or local) crime.

"I've got to get legislation passed by Congress to save America," White recalled Roosevelt saying. "If I come out for the anti-lynching bill now, [the southerners] will block every bill I ask Congress to pass to keep America from collapsing. I just can't take that risk." At that point, White, who had more than once risked his life in his crusade against lynching, could argue no further with the president of the United States.

For all his reluctance to take political risks, Roosevelt seemed to have more sympathy for black Americans than any president in memory, especially his two Republican predecessors. FDR, as he was often called, had even discussed ending racial discrimination in federal agencies—a highly radical proposal for

the time. And although some of his programs were worse than ineffective for black people, some of them, notably the Federal Emergency Relief Administration (FERA), proved of significant help. Roosevelt and the Democrats, many black men and women concluded, were not so bad—especially compared to the Republicans and their 1936 candidate, the ultraconservative governor of Kansas, Alfred M. Landon.

To Frederick Douglass, the Republican party had been "the ship"; after 1932, observes historian Lerone Bennett, Jr. (in *Before the Mayflower: A History of the Negro in America*, 1964), "Negro voters abandoned the ship and dived into the sea." Black people should "go home and turn Lincoln's picture to the wall," said Robert L. Vann, editor and publisher of the influential black newspaper *Pittsburgh Courier*. "The debt has

Young African Americans protest the absence of lynching on the agenda of a 1934 national conference on crime. Each of the demonstrators wears a noose carrying the name of a murdered black American.

been paid in full." As it turned out, the election of 1932 marked the end of the Republicans' grip on the black political soul. In 1936, 76 percent of African Americans abandoned their traditional party and voted for Roosevelt.

Even before this electoral thunderbolt, trend watchers had spotted a change in the political weather. In 1928, voters from Chicago's predominantly black South Side had sent a city councilman, black Republican Oscar DePriest, to Congress. In 1934, those voters made a switch: they replaced DePriest with Arthur W. Mitchell, also a black politician—but a Democrat, and the first African American of his party ever seated in the U.S. House of Representatives. Significantly, Mitchell's victory was credited to his slogan—"Forward with Roosevelt"—and his pro–New Deal stance.

But along with progress for black Americans, the 1930s brought setbacks and examples of American racism as searing as any in the nation's history. Rather than appreciating the political strength added by their party's new black members, southern Democrats recoiled. Delegates at the 1936 Democratic National Convention, for example, long remembered the entrance of South Carolina senator "Cotton Ed" Smith. As he ambled toward the podium, Smith looked up and froze in his tracks: delivering the meeting's opening prayer was an *African American* clergyman. "By God, he's as black as melted midnight!" screeched the South Carolinian. "This mongrel meeting ain't no place for a white man!" With that, Smith bolted from the auditorium.

Smothered laughter reportedly swept the hall as the outraged lawmaker hustled out. But few Americans, white or black, could smile at the merciless racism of such southern leaders as Mississippi's Senator Theodore Bilbo. In the 1930s, Germany's increasingly powerful Nazi leader, Adolf Hitler, began spreading his theories about a "master race." According to Hitler, only blond, blue-eyed "Aryans" had rights, a chilling concept that would result in the murder of millions of defenseless people, most of them Jews and other minorities. Bilbo sang his praises.

"Consider Germany," he said. "It is beginning to be recognized by the thoughtful minds of our age that the conservation of racial values is the only hope for future civilization." To further promote "racial values," Bilbo tried to get Congress to appropriate $1 billion to pay for the forced transport of all America's black citizens to Africa. He failed, but not before a large number of influential southerners had approved the plan.

Even grimmer racism showed up in a dark episode that began in Macon County, Alabama. There, in 1932, U.S. Public Health Service (PHS) officials initiated a major study of syphilis, a sexually transmitted disease that can cause paralysis, blindness, insanity, and heart failure. For the subjects of its program—entitled the Tuskegee Study of Untreated Syphilis in the Male Negro—the PHS recruited 622 black men, all of them poor, and the majority illiterate. Of these men, 431 had advanced cases of syphilis; the rest were free of the disease and served as controls (individuals included as a basis for comparison).

The Tuskegee Study was called a treatment program, but it turned out to be a human experiment, designed to chart the progression and development of a potentially fatal disease. To gain the trust of the men, most of them sharecroppers, the government doctors centered their work at Alabama's Tuskegee Institute, a black institution widely respected by black Americans. To further gain the trust of the project's black subjects, its directors hired a black nurse, Eunice Rivers. She told the men that they had "bad blood" and needed special treatment. Although the drug penicillin, which can cure the disease, became available in the 1940s, the sharecroppers never received it. Instead, they were given placebos (harmless but ineffective substances), which they were told would make them better.

Initially the Tuskegee Study was to last only six months to a year, but its duration was extended again and again. The men were given regular physical examinations, which included painful lumbar punctures (the insertion of needles into the spinal cord in order to obtain fluid for diagnosis). The punctures often caused the men severe headaches; in a few isolated cases, the procedure caused paralysis and even death of the subjects.

For almost 40 years, Tuskegee Study doctors gave their patients regular physical examinations. They kept careful records of the men's health and performed autopsies on those who died, but they never treated them for syphilis. So little understood was the Tuskegee Study that its subjects not only remained in the program but told friends of their good fortune in being selected; they were proud of the physical examinations—a luxury almost no sharecropper could have afforded on his own—enjoyed the hot lunches the study provided on examination days, and appreciated the burial allowance the government guaranteed their families. Eventually, in fact, more men volunteered as subjects than the study could accommodate.

The medical community was kept informed about the Tuskegee experiment, but the general public learned of it only in 1972, when an Associated Press reporter broke the story. The news sent a wave of shocked revulsion across the nation. Senator Edward Kennedy of Massachusetts, for example, labeled the study "an outrageous and intolerable situation which this government never should have been involved in." Finally, a black civil rights activist and lawyer, Fred D. Gray of Alabama, sued the U.S. government on behalf of the study's participants. Before the case could go to court, the government made a $9 million settlement to the Tuskegee survivors and the descendants of those who had died.

The story that shocked Americans of all races in 1972 was known only to a handful of nonmedical people in 1936. These included the experiment's participants and their friends and families—people who regarded it not as an extreme example of racism but as a benefit they were lucky to have.

Even without understanding Tuskegee, however, America's black population had more than enough examples of bigotry—some of it violent, even murderous—to convince them that a white politician who did not openly support white supremacy was better than one who did. The president appeared to be such a man, and by 1936, increasing numbers of black men and women supported him. In the case of some, however, the Roosevelt they voted for was Eleanor.

First Lady Eleanor Roosevelt was a compassionate, intelligent woman who hated to see truth swept under the rug. She made no effort, for example, to conceal the fact that some of her close friends were black people, and that she considered them fellow human beings who were unjustly deprived of their rights as American citizens. Walter White was one of Roosevelt's friends, although his single-minded concentration on his goals once provoked her into calling him "a great nuisance." However, she had continued, "if I were colored, I think I should have about the same obsession he has."

Eleanor Roosevelt's black friends included not only White but also pioneer educator and civil rights activist Mary McLeod Bethune. One of 17 children in a family of South Carolina sharecroppers and former slaves, Bethune was born in 1875. After a difficult struggle, she obtained an education and became a teacher; in 1904, she opened her own school, the Daytona [Florida] Normal and Industrial Institute for

Mary McLeod Bethune (center, in hat) takes leave of students at Bethune-Cookman College in 1943. By this time, the tireless educator, social worker, government administrator, and civil rights activist had become one of the nation's best-known women.

Negro Girls. Starting out almost penniless, Bethune managed to win local support from both blacks and whites, and her school flourished. After merging with the Cookman Institute [for black men] in 1923, the school changed its name to Bethune-Cookman College, eventually gaining full accreditation and a student body of more than 1,000 women and men.

A dedicated worker for education and racial harmony, Bethune became one of the best-known women in America. In 1935, she won the NAACP's Spingarn Medal, a coveted award given annually for "the highest or noblest achievement by an American Negro." Later that year, she founded the National Council of Negro Women. In 1936, President Roosevelt appointed her administrative assistant for Negro affairs of the National Youth Administration (NYA). A depression-born agency created to fight the high unemployment among young Americans, the

NYA paid people between the ages of 16 and 24 for participating in relief work and job-training programs.

Bethune's work in the NYA so impressed the president that in 1936 he created a new department, the Division of Negro Affairs. He appointed Bethune director, making her the first black woman to serve as the chief of a federal agency. Under her influence, the NYA became, in the words of one expert, "a model of government assistance for blacks."

As a special White House adviser on black affairs, Bethune joined an informal but exclusive club known as the Black Cabinet. Also called the Black Brain Trust, it was an informal group of prominent black citizens who occupied administrative posts in the New Deal—the first administration to tap the strengths of the nation's black intellectuals and professionals. Other members of the Black Cabinet included newspaper publisher Robert Vann (special assistant to the U.S. attorney general) and attorney William Hastie (assistant solicitor to the Department of the Interior and later, governor of the U.S. Virgin Islands and the first black judge on a U.S. circuit court of appeals).

Another Black Cabinet member, economist Robert Weaver, served as adviser to the Federal Housing Administration. (In 1966, President Lyndon Johnson would appoint Weaver secretary of the Department of Housing and Urban Development, making him the first black person in any president's official cabinet.) Social worker Lawrence Oxley served as New Deal chief of the Division of Negro Labor in the Department of Labor, and poet, physician, and educator Frank Horne (uncle of entertainer Lena Horne) worked as adviser to several federal agencies, most of them involving housing.

As director of Negro Affairs for the NYA, Bethune traveled around the country, campaigning for better education for black Americans. Her speaking engagements often meshed with those of the first lady, with whom she had begun a lifelong friendship in 1927. Although Eleanor Roosevelt had been born to wealth and privilege, her compassion and concern for her fellow humans ran deep. Bethune, born to grinding poverty and limited horizons, shared Roosevelt's way of thinking. Because Roosevelt was willing to learn and Bethune ready to teach, the United States took several long steps toward racial justice.

In 1934, after years of absorbing Bethune's wisdom, Roosevelt addressed a conference on black education. "The day of working together has come, and we must learn to work together, all of us, regardless of race or creed or color," she said. "We go ahead together or we go down together." Bethune, in fact, had done such a good job of educating her receptive pupil about black people and their problems that it was often Eleanor, not Franklin, to whom black leaders turned when they needed government help or cooperation. In the end, observed Roy Wilkins of the NAACP, the president depended on his wife to "run interference" on "the Negro question."

Eleanor Roosevelt also played a key role in an astonishing drama that unfolded in Washington, D.C., in 1939. The cast of characters included Walter White, Secretary of State Harold Ickes, black contralto Marian Anderson, and a group of white American women who called themselves the Daughters of the American Revolution (DAR). Anderson's rare talent ("Yours is a voice," said the great conductor Arturo Toscanini, "one hears once in a hundred years") and calm courage in the face of blatant racism led the NAACP to announce her as the winner of its 1939 Spingarn Medal.

To celebrate the upcoming award, Anderson's manager decided to stage a concert in Washington's Constitution Hall, a magnificent space owned by the DAR. When he wrote for a reservation, however, the DAR turned him down; their hall, they said, was unavailable to Miss Anderson on the requested date (Easter Sunday)—or on any other date. The DAR had never accepted black members; now it proved that it accepted no black artists, either.

The response was immediate and explosive. Eleanor Roosevelt very publicly resigned from the DAR. Mayor Fiorello La Guardia of New York thundered, "No hall is too good for Marian Anderson!" Renowned violinist Jascha Heifetz refused to set foot in the DAR concert space. Instead of peforming at Constitution Hall, Marian Anderson agreed to give a free public concert. Walter White scheduled it for Easter Sunday. Harold Ickes approved use of the Lincoln Memorial. When the day arrived, a record crowd—75,000 Americans of all races—faced the statue of the white man who had freed the slaves 76 years earlier and honored a black woman known as the "voice of the American soul."

In the 1930s, many signs suggested that America's racial problems were worsening. But some events gave heart to the nation's peacemakers. The Anderson concert was one of them. When the contralto finished her last song, "Nobody Knows the Trouble I've Seen," the audience sat in absolute silence, then broke into an earsplitting roar and rushed forward. From the podium, Walter White saw a young black woman stretching her arms toward Anderson. Her hands, he later recalled, "despite their youth, had known only the dreary work of manual labor." Her face streamed with tears, but in her eyes, said White, "flamed hope bordering on ecstasy. . . . If Marian Anderson could do it, the girl's eyes seemed to say, then I can, too."

3

NEW FRONTIERS:
COLLEGES, COURTS, AND
BALLOT BOXES

The National Association for the Advancement of Colored People was founded in 1909. During its first 20 years, the organization concentrated on three main goals: putting an end to racial violence, securing black voting rights, and eliminating discrimination in housing and public places. By the early 1930s, however, priorities had begun to shift. NAACP officials realized that, to reach the original goals, black Americans would first need social and economic equality—which would, in turn, require educational equality. Education, then, became the cornerstone; without it, asserted the NAACP, black people might never secure their rightful share in America's prizes.

The organization's next move: a meticulously planned, hard-hitting campaign to open the nation's school and college doors to all citizens. At this point in American history—the 1930s—no educational institution, *public or private*, had a legal obligation to accept any student its directors did not want. As a

An official at the NAACP's New York City headquarters points to the group's new recruitment poster in the mid-1930s. During these years, the civil rights organization mobilized a vigorous campaign to desegregate institutes of higher education.

result, southern schools (as well as many in the North) were strictly segregated by race. The legality of this state of affairs rested on *Plessy v. Ferguson,* an 1896 Supreme Court decision that established an important policy called "separate but equal."

The Court's decision had involved a black southerner, Homer Adolph Plessy. In 1892, he bought a first-class ticket, boarded a Louisiana train, and sat down in the car reserved for whites. Reminding him that the law required people of color to use the segregated "Jim Crow" car, the conductor ordered Plessy to move. ("Jim Crow" began with the 19th century's popular minstrel shows, which often featured white comic actors wearing "blackface" and dancing to the refrain, "Jump, Jim Crow!" The term came to be used both as a patronizing name for black people and as a descriptive phrase for post–Civil War segregation.) Plessy, however, did not care for Jim Crow's company; he insisted on occupying the seat he had paid for.

In so doing, he violated an 1890 Louisiana law calling for "equal but separate accommodations for the white and colored races" in public places. He was arrested, tried, and found guilty by Louisiana judge John H. Ferguson. Plessy appealed, and in 1896, his case wound up in U.S. Supreme Court. A majority of justices upheld Ferguson: they ruled that the Constitution's Fourteenth Amendment, which guaranteed all citizens "equal protection of the laws," required accommodations to be equal but not necessarily identical.

Citing the "separate but equal" doctrine, courts routinely dismissed antisegregation suits from that point on. Black southern students could be compelled to attend segregated schools as long as local authorities—who were almost invariably white—deemed these schools "equal" to those reserved for whites. Legally equal they may have been, but there the balance ended; in practice, southern school districts spent only a fraction as much money on black schools as on white. Segregation—and all it implied—had become the law of the land.

This "law" was the NAACP's principal target. Aware that white southerners were highly sensitive about racial matters relating to their young children, organization strategists decided to aim first at what they considered the "soft underbelly" of the educational system: graduate schools, law schools in particular. NAACP officials believed that judges, who were lawyers themselves, might quickly grasp the argument that "separate"—and therefore underfunded, understaffed, and undersupplied—law schools could never be "equal." Spearheading the NAACP campaign would be attorneys who had been specifically trained to use U.S. law to secure black rights. Fortunately for the NAACP—and for the future of all African Americans—the organization included some of the most innovative legal minds the 20th century has produced.

The 1930s and 1940s were crucial decades for the approximately 1,000 African American lawyers in the United States. This was a period of reassessment and reaffirmation, years that witnessed the rise of a more militant definition of the black lawyer's proper role. Increased racial awareness and larger numbers of black lawyers eager and well trained in civil rights law coincided with the emergence of a more liberal and sympathetic United States Supreme Court. Thus the stage was set for an especially effective legal challenge to racial discrimination and segregation.

Charles Hamilton Houston, vice dean of the Howard University School of Law, works at his desk in 1939. Houston encouraged students to work for civil rights: "What Charlie beat into our heads," recalled Thurgood Marshall, "was excellence."

That challenge was led by **Charles Hamilton Houston, special counsel to the NAACP's national legal committee. A Washington, D.C.–born civil rights activist, Houston graduated from Amherst [Massachusetts] College at the age** of 19 in 1915. After earning a law degree from Harvard University, he joined the faculty of Howard University School of Law. He served as its vice dean from 1929 to 1935 and then became NAACP special counsel. Under Houston's leadership the Howard law school, as one historian put it, "became a living laboratory where civil rights law was invented by teamwork." As a law professor, Houston trained—and inspired—a small army of young black attorneys, all of them tough, creative, and determined to reshape history.

Among this group was William Henry Hastie, a brilliant young Tennessean who had earned high praise at Harvard. One of his professors, future Supreme Court justice Felix Frankfurter, had said Hastie was "not only the best colored man we have ever had, but as good as all but three or four outstanding white men that have been [at Harvard law school] during the last 20 years." Born in 1904 in Knoxville, Hastie had earned his bachelor's degree in 1925 from Amherst College, Houston's own alma mater. After graduating from Harvard in 1930, Hastie joined Houston on the faculty of Howard law school, where he remained for seven years. During that period, the Roosevelt administration tapped him as assistant solicitor in the U.S. Department of the Interior.

In 1937, Roosevelt placed Hastie on the U.S. District Court for the U.S. Virgin Islands, making him the nation's first black federal judge. Two years later, Hastie returned to Howard as dean of the law school. Taking a leave of absence in 1940 (the year before the outbreak of World War II), he became a civilian aide to the U.S. secretary of war, but in 1943, he quit to protest ongoing segregation in the armed forces. He returned to Howard, where he taught law until President Harry S. Truman appointed him governor of the

Virgin Islands. In 1949, Truman appointed him judge of the U.S. Court of Appeals for the Third Circuit, where he served with distinction until his retirement in 1971.

Another extraordinary Houston protégé was Thurgood Marshall, great-grandson of an enslaved Congolese man brought to America in the mid-1800s. Born in 1908 in West Baltimore, Maryland, Marshall graduated from Pennyslvania's Lincoln University, America's oldest black college, in 1930. After the University of Maryland law school rejected him because of his race, Marshall entered Howard, graduating at the top

Taking the oath of office as judge of the U.S. Court of Appeals, Third Circuit, in 1949, William Henry Hastie becomes the nation's first African American to hold a federal judgeship.

of his law class in 1933. The following year, he joined Houston at the NAACP. Together, these two men would form one of the most effective teams in American civil rights history.

Recalling Houston years later, Marshall said, "Charlie's phrase was social engineer. He wanted the lawyer to take over the leadership in the community." Long after he received his law degree, Marshall gave a group of black law students some advice: "When you get into a courtroom, you can't just say, 'Please, Mr. Court, have mercy on me because I'm a Negro.' You are in competition with a well-trained white lawyer and you better be at least as good as he is; and if you expect to win, you better be better."

Charles Houston and Thurgood Marshall scored their first big court victory in 1935. The case (*Murray v. Pearson*) pitted Donald Murray, a 20-year-old black college graduate, against the University of Maryland and its president, Raymond Pearson. Murray, who was well qualified, twice applied to the Maryland law school; Pearson twice rejected him. "The university," he said flatly, "does not accept Negro students." Murray, added Pearson, could get just as good an education at a nearby all-black college. At this point, Murray appealed to the NAACP: Houston and Marshall took the case to court, where they forced Pearson to admit that the black school offered no legal degree, that Murray met all the requirements for the University of Maryland, and that the university was the only institution that could train Murray in Maryland law.

Concluding his team's argument, Marshall asserted that Pearson himself had proven that the university was legally bound to accept Murray. "What's at stake here is more than the rights of my client," he said. "It's the moral commitment stated in our country's creed." To the delighted astonishment of the

NAACP team and its supporters, the Baltimore city court agreed. The university appealed, but the state court of appeals upheld the verdict. Murray entered the university, earned his law degree, and opened his own practice. Throughout his subsequent career, Murray made his legal services available to the NAACP; not surprisingly, he never asked for a fee.

In 1936, Marshall and Houston again enlisted their legal skills against a white educational bastion. This time, the battleground was the segregated law school of the University of Missouri, and the client a young black college graduate named Lloyd Gaines. Openly rejecting Gaines because of his race, the uni-

Thurgood Marshall (left) and Charles Houston (right) work with Donald Gaines Murray (center) on their historic 1935 lawsuit against the University of Maryland. The Murray case was to be the NAACP's first major school-desegregation victory.

Gathered for a 1930s portrait are some of the NAACP legal warriors who gave Jim Crow his death blows. In the front row are Walter White (left) and Edward P. Lovett; in back are (left to right) James G. Tyson, Leon A. Ransom, and Charles Houston.

versity offered to pay his tuition at an out-of-state law school. This plan, asserted Missouri officials, complied with the "separate but equal" doctrine. The NAACP attorneys emphatically disagreed. Representing Gaines, they argued that if the university refused to accept Gaines, it was obliged to provide him with an equal legal education within the state. They lost a series of suits against the university in Missouri courts, but in 1938, the U.S. Supreme Court agreed to hear the case.

Once again, Houston's nimble legal mind and Marshall's dazzling eloquence won the day. The Supreme Court ruled against Missouri, agreeing with the lawyers' argument that "separate" was permissible only when it was also truly "equal." Gaines never attended law school in Missouri, having enrolled at the University of Michigan during the long legal fight. Nevertheless, his case achieved far more than a single victory against one segregated school. From this point on, southern states would either have to integrate their law schools or build and staff brand-new schools just for black students—an expense no state was prepared to meet.

The victory left Marshall, Houston, and other NAACP officials jubilant. One day in the future, they predicted, the Supreme Court might extend this view to public schools at all levels; on that day, black children would have as many books, teachers, and facilities as white children, and black teachers would receive the same salaries for the same work.

Murray and *Gaines* were the first steps in a long journey that would eventually end in triumph. In case after case, the NAACP, for the most part led by the courageous Marshall, would hammer one nail after another into the coffins of *Plessy v. Ferguson,* the doctrine of "separate but equal," and Jim Crow himself.

When Houston returned to private law practice in 1938, Marshall assumed his position as NAACP special counsel. The following year, NAACP chief Walter White created a new branch of the organization: the Legal Defense and Educational Fund (usually called simply "the Fund"), a body that would provide free legal aid to blacks who suffered injustice because of their race. Appointed director-counsel of the Fund was Thurgood Marshall.

During the next 20 years, Marshall would argue 32 cases before the Supreme Court and win 27 of them. His work would help move a reluctant, segregationist nation toward racial justice by going to court and battling for black rights in schools, voting booths, criminal courts, public facilities, and housing. He would become a federal judge in 1962, U.S. solicitor general in 1965, and, in 1967, the first black justice of the U.S. Supreme Court, a position he was to hold until shortly before his death in 1993.

The herculean efforts of Marshall, Houston, Hastie, and White, along with a host of other NAACP legal warriors—including Edward P. Lovett, James G. Tyson, Conrad Pearson, Cecil McCoy, Raymond Pace Alexander, Leon A. Ransom, and James M. Nabrit—eventually gained national fame. But also vital to the organization was the devoted work of black women around the nation. Working in their own neighborhoods, an army of unsung women initiated countless membership drives, raised funds, and built local branches into state federations. On the national level, too, black women served in many important capacities. Among this vast and impressive sisterhood were Mary Burnett Talbert (1866–1923), Daisy Adams Lampkin (c.1844–1965), and Juanita Jackson Mitchell (1913–1992).

Born in Oberlin, Ohio, Mary Burnett graduated from Oberlin College, one of the first educational institutions to admit blacks and women. After spending five years as a teacher in the segregated schools of Little Rock, Arkansas, she married realtor William H. Talbert and moved to Buffalo, New York. There, she joined the Phillis Wheatley Club, an activist black women's group that built a settlement house for the city's underprivileged people. As the club's president, Talbert affiliated it with the influential National Association of Colored Women (NACW); in 1910, she invited the fledgling NAACP to organize a chapter in Buffalo.

From 1916 to 1920 Talbert served as president of the NACW, which she represented at an international meeting of women's groups held in Norway in 1920. A writer, lecturer, educator, and fiercely vocal opponent of lynching, Talbert served as a NAACP vice president from 1918 until her death in 1923. She greatly strengthened the organization by organizing chapters in Louisiana and Texas, and in 1922, she became the first woman to win the NAACP's coveted Spingarn Medal.

Daisy Adams, Talbert's contemporary and fellow activist, was born in Washington, D.C. She graduated from high school in Reading, Pennsylvania, then moved to Pittsburgh, where she married William Lampkin in 1912. In 1915 she became president of the Negro Women's Franchise League, a group dedicated to obtaining the vote for women (a goal achieved in 1920). Lampkin proved herself an extraordinarily effective fund-raiser. During World War I, she directed Liberty Bond sales in the black community of Pennsylvania's Allegheny County, selling some $2 million worth of the government securities. In 1930, Walter White enlisted her as regional field secretary of the NAACP, a post she held until she was made national field secretary in 1935.

As an NAACP executive, Lampkin continued to demonstrate her gift for raising money; she also enlisted large numbers of new members in the civil rights organization. (Despite her formidable financial skills, she never raised money for herself, and accepted only a modest salary from the NAACP.) Lampkin played leadership roles in the National Council of Negro Women (NCNW) and the National Association of Colored Women (NACW), and was also active in politics. She personally helped defeat a number of racist legislators, including senators Roscoe McCullough of Ohio and Henry J. Allen of Kansas.

Lampkin's death at the age of 81 in 1965 brought forth an outpouring of praise. Speaking for many Americans, Pennsylvania governor Dick Thornburgh said, "Daisy Lampkin courageously sought full equality for blacks and women throughout the country. Today her work stands as an inspiration for countless citizens."

Juanita E. Jackson was born in 1913 in Hot Springs, Arkansas, and raised in Baltimore, Maryland. She obtained a degree in education from the University of Pennsylvania in 1931, then returned to Baltimore, where she hoped to help heal the depression-scarred lives of the city's African Americans. Believing that a forum—where young people could freely discuss and plan attacks on such scourges as unemployment, segregation, and lynching—was the best starting point, Jackson founded just such an institution: the City-Wide Young People's Forum of Baltimore. The success of the group, which Jackson headed from 1931 to 1934, brought her to the attention of NAACP chief Walter White. She accepted White's offer of leadership of the civil rights organization's new youth program, and from 1935 to 1938, she served as NAACP national youth director.

In 1938, Jackson married fellow civil rights activist Clarence Mitchell, with whom she would have four sons. While raising her family, Juanita Mitchell also managed to coordinate a 2,000-person civil rights march, participate in a White House conference on children, direct an NAACP voter-registration campaign in Baltimore, and, in 1950, earn a law degree from the University of Maryland. Becoming the first black woman admitted to practice law in Maryland, Mitchell embarked on a series of landmark cases that helped destroy racial segregation on the state's public beaches as well as in its public schools. Juanita Mitchell remained unceasingly active, directing voter campaigns, presiding over the local NAACP branch, and chairing the legal committee of the NCNW. On her death at the age of 79 in 1992, she was hailed by

NAACP director Benjamin Hooks as "one of the greatest freedom fighters in the history of Maryland and the nation."

The New Deal era witnessed the appearance of a growing number of northern blacks to high-ranking office. Crystal Bird Fauset of Philadelphia became the first black woman to be elected to the Pennsylvania House of Representatives. A year later, New York City mayor Fiorello La Guardia appointed Jane Matilda Bolin to the Court of Domestic Relations, an act that made Bolin the first black female judge in U.S. history.

In another significant breakthrough, Dr. Louis T. Wright became the first black physician to attain a major position in medical administration: he was appointed surgical director at New York City's Harlem Hospital in 1943. A graduate of Harvard Medical School, Wright was a distinguished figure in American medicine and surgery for more than two decades.

Black advances in winning elective offices and appointed positions were, along with an array of favorable U.S. Supreme Court decisions, welcome signs of racial progress. But for the majority of blacks, who found themselves at the bottom of the socioeconomic scale, such fundamental issues as jobs and housing commanded far more attention. Meanwhile, the masses of black Americans found temporary relief from the ravages of the depression and the persistent discrimination and segregation by creating and participating in a rich and fluid popular culture.

4

FROM BOJANGLES TO BIGGER: THE RISE OF BLACK POPULAR CULTURE

In hard economic times, people yearn for a brighter world; popular culture responds with fantasy and spectacle. Not surprisingly, then, the extraordinarily bleak American 1930s produced an especially dazzling display of music, film, and athletic prowess.

In heartland America, radio was king (television was still more than a decade in the future). In increasing numbers Americans of all races and ages glued themselves to their favorite radio programs, weeping for hard-pressed soap-opera martyrs, roaring over favorite comics, breathlessly absorbing dramas, cheering for home teams. Outside the home, Americans flocked to the movies and flooded into sports arenas. Mostly inexpensive and easily accessible, these activities seemed to make deprivation and adversity a little easier to bear.

African Americans endured the same widespread poverty, joblessness, and hunger as whites did. But black men and women also had to bear special, additional crosses: entrenched discrimination and segre-

---

Duke Ellington (right, standing) swings with his orchestra in 1942, a time when he was at the peak of his creativity and renown. Black entertainers in general had reached new heights of popularity in the 1930s and 1940s.

gation. Everywhere they turned, black people saw and heard absurd caricatures and mockeries of themselves: negative, stereotyped images of black Americans appeared on postcards, cereal boxes, cookie jars, lunch boxes. Well-to-do white families decorated their lawns with statues of servile black jockeys; whites addressed railroad porters, waiters, hotel bellmen, and other service workers—of any age—as "Boy." Elderly southern blacks were called "Uncle" and "Aunt" by patronizing whites; northern blacks called whites "Mrs." and "Mr." while they were themselves uniformly addressed by their first names. Segregation ruled, by law in some areas, by custom in others. Blacks and whites used largely segregated schools, theaters, beaches, restaurants, hotels, and other public facilities.

For white audiences, "darkie" humor could be counted on for laughs, and it appeared often in movies and on the radio. Insulting and degrading stereotypes made black people appear to be less than human, and African Americans naturally looked for more accurate images of themselves. For such images, many turned to sports; others escaped into the great protest novels of the day, or became devoted fans of various black entertainers and film stars. Black singers, musicians, comedians, actors, baseball players, track stars, novelists, and painters—many of them unknown to whites—attained superstar status in segregated neighborhoods across the land. Black patronage enabled an array of cultural celebrities to enjoy status and prestige rarely accorded people of color. The rich cultural legacy that black people fashioned during the depression years provides an impressive example of African American survival strategies and rising racial consciousness.

Among the best-known of the depression era's black icons was Bill "Bojangles" Robinson (1878–1949). Born in Richmond, Virginia, and

orphaned as an infant, Robinson began his career at the age of six, when he danced for pennies in Richmond saloons. By the time he was eight, he had hitched a ride to Washington, D.C., and landed a job as a stableboy. From his fellow workers, he learned such fashionable dance steps as the buck-and-wing, and he soon developed his own series of elaborate routines. Robinson began dancing in vaudeville shows, steadily gaining popularity. He appeared on New York City's Broadway in *Blackbirds of 1928* and *Brown Buddies* (1930), then moved on to Hollywood.

As Bill Bojangles, Robinson became one of America's most popular black entertainers, but with success came controversy. Many black Americans criticized him for his stage persona, which they characterized as that of an "Uncle Tom." Ambivalent reception notwithstanding, Robinson enjoyed a remarkable career in the movies. Like most other American institutions, however, the Hollywood film industry practiced rigid racial discrimination, offering black actors and actresses few roles except those of the grinning clown or the sassy servant.

For all his greatness, Robinson's career was circumscribed by these racial realities. Still, from 1929 to 1943, he performed in 14 Hollywood films and produced a number of all-black features for black audiences. He was most famous for his film appearances with wildly popular white child star Shirley Temple; Robinson-Temple movies included *The Little Colonel* (1935), *The Littlest Rebel* (1935), and *Rebecca of Sunnybrook Farm* (1938). Black movie critic Donald Bogle has written that "one of the finest moments in the history of musical American movies remains the one in which Bill Robinson teaches Shirley Temple how to dance up the magic staircase in *The Little Colonel*." At the height of his career on the stage and screen, the internationally celebrated Robinson commanded fees as high as $6,500 for a single performance. Such a sum—far more than the annual income of many poor black citizens—made Robinson seem almost superhuman to his public.

Bill "Bojangles" Robinson, sometimes called "the Satrap of Tap," teaches child star Shirley Temple his famous stair dance in the 1935 film The Little Colonel. *Robinson met with some criticism for playing subservient characters, but no one could deny his remarkable talent as a dancer.*

The era also produced the incomparable jazz singer Billie Holiday (1915–1959). "Lady Day," as she was widely known, was born Eleanora Fagan in Baltimore,

Maryland. As a teenager, she listened to the records of the great contemporary blues and jazz musicians—such artists as singer Bessie Smith and trumpeter Louis Armstrong—and, from humble and often traumatic beginnings, went on to become one of the century's most accomplished jazz singers herself.

Holiday made her professional singing debut at the age of 15, singing for tips in a Harlem speakeasy (a bar where liquor was sold during Prohibition, the period between 1920 and 1933, when the sale and consumption of alcoholic beverages were outlawed in the United States). At 18, Holiday was "discovered" by jazz producer and promoter John Hammond, who later said simply, "She was the best jazz singer I had ever heard." In 1933 Hammond arranged her first recording (with clarinetist Benny Goodman), and in 1935 she performed for a tremendously receptive audience at Harlem's Apollo Theater, arguably the most important black entertainment center in America. Throughout the 1930s she sang with the Count Basie and Artie Shaw bands.

A brilliant, highly individualistic singer who used her voice as an instrument, Holiday had the ability to move even the hardest heart. "That woman," remarked one critic, "could sing the telephone book and make you cry." But she was also deeply troubled, falling victim to both drugs and liquor. At 44—her voice still astonishing, but her body destroyed by abuse—she died in a Manhattan hospital. She left behind her a vast army of devoted fans and a unique catalog of records. One of her most powerful and best-known songs was "Strange Fruit," recorded in 1939. A heartbreaking, shocking lament for black lynch victims, the song became her signature.

Coinciding with the rise of Billie Holiday was the birth of the Swing Age, a time when big bands, many of them headed by black musicians, scored impressive commercial success. Among the most notable big

Billie Holiday performs at New York City's celebrated jazz club Jimmy Ryan's in 1942. "That woman," remarked one admirer, "could sing the telephone book and make you cry."

bands were those led by Count Basie, Cab Calloway, and Duke Ellington.

Other African American performers who found themselves in the limelight during the 1930s included popular actresses Louise Beavers (1902–1962) and Hattie McDaniel (1895–1952). Beavers won both considerable fame and substantial criticism for her work in *Imitation of Life*, a 1934 film based on a novel by Fannie Hurst. In this sentimental drama, Beavers plays Delilah, the long-suffering but understanding mother of a beautiful, light-skinned daughter who passes for white, played by Fredi Washington.

Both Beavers and Washington were acclaimed for their sensitive performances, but both suffered criticism for allegedly helping to reinforce the idea that all light-skinned black men and women yearned to be white. Undaunted, both continued to practice their art. Washington often earned flattering notices on the New York stage, and she also worked toward equal rights, helping to found the Negro Actors Guild and serving as secretary for an actors' committee that attempted to secure equal hotel accommodations for black actors.

Beavers went on to play what one critic called "innumerable happy housekeepers," appearing in more than 100 movies, including *She Done Him Wrong*, with her good friend Mae West (1933), *The Last Gangster* (1937), *Brother Rat* (1938), and *Made for Each Other* (1939). In the 1952–53 television season, she played the title role in *Beulah*, a comedy series.

Among the racial stereotypes most despised by black Americans was that of the headscarf-wearing, obese, dutiful mammy. This figure, however, appealed to white Americans, with their romanticized images of black women who preferred nurturing white families to caring for their own. The mammy role, therefore, was often a fixture in Hollywood scripts—and usually the only part calling for an actress of color.

In 1939, when actress Hattie McDaniel won the role of Mammy in the epic film *Gone with the Wind*, some black leaders criticized her as a "female Tom," but others praised her for the accomplishment. They knew that the servant role was about the only one available to black actresses, and they also knew that Mammy in *GWTW*, as the film came to be called, was a choice role.

McDaniel's humorous, tough, proud Mammy made her the first African American, male or female, ever to win an Academy Award (she received the Oscar for Best Supporting Actress). But she also received something less pleasant: a sharp reprimand from Walter White. The outspoken NAACP leader reproached not only

McDaniel but performers Louise Beavers, Stepin Fetchit (born Lincoln Theodore Monroe Andrew Perry), and Clarence Muse, for accepting servile roles. In response to this criticism, McDaniel and other black actors formed the Fair Play Committee (FPC), a group aimed at persuading the movie industry to offer black men and women more substantial roles and to eliminate such offensive terms as "nigger." The FPC made little headway, but McDaniel's career success continued: by 1947, she was starring in the very popular radio show *Beulah,* originating the role later taken over by Louise Beavers on television.

In Hollywood, black actors had a choice: accept the roles offered them or not work. But not all filmmaking took place in Hollywood, and not all of it was in white hands. Oscar Micheaux (pronounced *mee-show*), an enterprising African American born in Illinois in 1884, had been a train porter, farmer, book publisher, cattle rancher, and novelist. In the 1920s, he became interested in movies, which he saw as a potential gold mine. His films, aimed primarily at the black middle class, showed a fantasy world in which black Americans were as educated, cultured, and prosperous as their white counterparts. In Micheaux's world, the difficulties faced by the black working class were far less important than such middle-class issues as passing for white.

Working in Chicago and New York City, Micheaux made 46 films—29 of them silent, the rest "talkies"—between 1920 and 1948. (To the great regret of film historians and fans, many Micheaux films have been lost.) In 1931, the enterprising producer released *The Exile,* the first sound motion picture to be made with, by, and for black Americans. A

subsequent movie, *Veiled Aristocrats* (1932), concentrated on the theme of passing for white in Chicago's well-educated and refined mulatto community. The characters are "aristocrats" because they are descended from the white gentry of the Old South and Europe; they are "veiled" because of their color. The plot turns on the revelation that the wealthy "white" heroine is actually "colored," which makes it possible for her to marry the talented mulatto hero.

Micheaux faced frequent criticism from other black Americans, who complained that some of his films showed black men shooting craps, drinking in sleazy bars, and fighting; these images, said one critic, were "not any too pleasing to those of us who desire to see the better side of Negro life portrayed." Sensi-

Mammy (Hattie McDaniel) tightens the corset of Scarlett O'Hara (Vivien Leigh) in a scene from the 1939 movie Gone with the Wind. *McDaniel's performance in the smash hit film garnered her an Academy Award— the first ever for an African American—for Best Supporting Actress.*

tive to such complaints, the producer defended himself in an essay published in the *Philadelphia Afro-American*:

> I have always tried to make my photo plays present the truth, to lay before the race a cross section of its own life, to view the colored heart from close range. . . . It is only by presenting those portions of the race portrayed in my pictures, in the light and background of their true state, that we can raise our people to greater heights. I am too much imbued with the spirit of Booker T. Washington to engraft false virtues upon ourselves, to make ourselves that which we are not. Nothing could be a greater blow to our own progress.

Micheaux, who played the role of the film impresario to the hilt—six feet tall and broad of build, he wore long Russian coats and flamboyant wide-brimmed hats—managed to get his films exhibited largely through the force of his personality. But he faced an uphill battle: the number of theaters that would even show black films was small, and his budgets were extremely tight. He went bankrupt, was refinanced by white investors, but finally gave up the business. He died on a book-promotion tour in 1951.

Micheaux's ultimate failure to gain the support of middle-class black Americans did not discourage others from aiming at the same market through different media. In 1942, for example, John Johnson launched *Ebony* magazine, a black periodical modeled after *Life* magazine. Johnson's publication celebrated the successes achieved by members of the black middle class and cultural elite.

Movie stars, musicians, and magazines surely helped to raise black morale, but it was black athletes who truly captured the heart of African America. Poor, disheartened black men and women identified with the victories of the era's great black athletes in a profoundly personal way. When a black athlete outperformed a white competitor, the average black person felt a thrill of vicarious triumph.

Baseball was especially popular in black communities. All through the depression, the Negro Baseball Leagues provided some of the best and most affordable entertainment available to black areas across the country. (Like many other areas of American life, baseball was strictly segregated; all the major league teams were exclusively white.) Black baseball teams were hard hit by the depression, and during the early 1930s, many either folded completely or survived only by passing the hat between innings. Despite the hard times, virtually every major black community had its own baseball team: Indianapolis, for example, had its ABCs, Pittsburgh its Homestead Grays, New York its Black Yankees. And as the economy improved during the 1940s, the outstanding talent of black players drew larger and larger crowds.

One of the most notable players of this era was Joshua "Josh" Gibson, considered by many baseball authorities to be the most powerful slugger in the sport's history. Born in 1911 in Buena Vista, Georgia, Gibson moved with his family to Pittsburgh, Pennsylvania, in 1923. After dropping out of school in the ninth grade, he began playing on an all-black amateur team, the Gimbels A. C. By the age of 15, Gibson had moved on to the semiprofessional Crawford Colored Giants of Pittsburgh, where his astonishing ability as a hitter quickly attracted attention.

Gibson's talent did not go unnoticed by the local Negro League team, the Homestead Grays, which added the promising youth to its top-ranked club in 1929. In 1931, the 20-year-old player was credited with 75 home runs, "feeding the growing legend," writes sports authority Robert Peterson, "about the young black catcher who could hit the ball a country mile." By 1932, Gibson was an established star, but plummeting gate receipts had impoverished the Grays, and Gibson was lured to a rival team, the Pittsburgh Crawfords. The owner of the Crawfords,

Gus Greenlee, was an ambitious Pittsburgh "business-man" who ran numbers and hijacked trucks in addition to putting together one of the finest baseball teams of all time. His team's roster included Oscar Charleston, Cool Papa Bell, Jimmy Crutchfield, and a fast-talking fastball pitcher from Alabama named Satchel Paige. Paige and Gibson formed what Peterson asserts was "perhaps the greatest battery in baseball history." The club dissolved five years later (thanks to a new reform-oriented city government that all but bankrupted Greenlee), but during its life span, Greenlee built his team its own park—the first baseball field owned by a black man.

Slugger Josh Gibson demonstrates his catcher's stance during his playing days (1932–37) with the Pittsburgh Crawfords. "He attacked the ball," said a fellow Negro leaguer of the power-hitting catcher—and, some experts say, baseball's all-time greatest batter—"He was as strong as two men."

In 1937, Gibson returned to the Homestead Grays, where, "for the next two years," notes Peterson, "Gibson's big bat was the piledriving punch on the strongest club in Negro baseball." A stroke killed the mighty slugger at the age of 36; the story of his career, however, will live as long as there are people who love America's national sport.

Baseball afforded one kind of diversion; boxing, another. The victory of a black boxer carried heavy symbolic weight, especially if his opponent was white. Joe Louis Barrow (1914–1981) was one of the greatest prizefighters in the history of the sport. The son of Alabama sharecroppers, he moved with his family to Detroit, Michigan, when he was 12. Young Joe's mother wanted him to be a violin player, but, as Louis biographer Robert Jakoubek put it, "He showed not the slightest aptitude for the instrument." When he was 18, a friend who was a 1932 Detroit Golden Gloves champion invited him to visit his gym and act as his sparring partner. Joe accepted, then landed a right that almost knocked his friend out of the ring. The friend grinned and said, "Man, throw that violin away!" From then on, Joe spent all his free time training in the ring.

In 1935, after a sensational string of early victories, Louis (he had dropped Barrow when he started fighting) found himself in New York City's Yankee Stadium, squared off against former world heavyweight champion Primo Carnera. Attended by a record crowd, the fight had international political overtones: Carnera was an Italian; Louis was African American. At that moment, the Fascist Italian government of dictator Benito Mussolini was threatening to invade Ethiopia, the world's oldest independent black nation, ruled by Emperor Haile Selassie, a great hero to many American blacks. The crowd—some 62,000 people—at the stadium, noted one sportswriter, was "composed largely of Italians . . . and Negroes." When

Louis defeated the gigantic Carnera in the sixth round, the police braced for trouble in the extremely partisan audience, but astonishingly, none came. *Everybody* cheered. "The whites," noted sportswriter Damon Runyon, "applauded the amazing performance of this youthful Negro more than the blacks."

A year after the Carnera fight, the "Brown Bomber," as Louis had been nicknamed, went up against Max Schmeling, the German former heavyweight champion. Schmeling knocked him out in the 12th round. Louis's setback was only temporary, however, and he came back to win the heavyweight title in 1937 from James J. Braddock, whom he knocked out in the eighth round. The next year, Louis finally avenged himself and his race when, to the great delight of millions of black radio listeners, he battered Schmeling to the canvas in one round. His victory raised black morale and confidence during the bleak depression years.

Black America had another unquestioned morale booster in sprinter Jesse Owens. Born in Oakville, Alabama, in 1913, Owens was raised in Cleveland, Ohio. His performance as a sprinter on his high school track team attracted the attention of his coaches, and while he was a student at Ohio State University his running earned him the nickname "Ebony Antelope." Participating in the 1936 Olympics in Berlin, Germany, Owens won an astounding four gold medals and broke the world record in the 100-yard dash. The Olympics had been staged that year with unusual pageantry; racist German dictator Adolf Hitler was determined that the athletic events would once and for all prove that "Aryans"—blond, blue-eyed northern Europe-

Max Schmeling (left) lands a left to Joe Louis's face during their 1936 match. Schmeling won this battle, but Louis came back two years later to defeat the German former heavyweight champion in a single spectacular round.

ans—constituted the world's superior race. After Jesse Owens made his historic 100-yard run, an aide asked Hitler to pose for a picture with the triumphant athlete. Hitler turned to him in fury. "Do you really think," he hissed, "that I will allow myself to be photographed shaking hands with a Negro?" Owens's astonishing Olympic performance, coupled with Hitler's ugly snub, made him an instant international superstar as well as a potent symbol of racial harmony. The achievements of the "Ebony Antelope" remain untarnished; most athletic experts continue to rate him as the greatest track-and-field athlete of the first half of the 20th century.

Although the exploits of black athletic performers dominated black America's imagination, black men and women in other arenas also made outstanding

Sprinter Jesse Owens crouches for a start during a workout at the 1936 Olympic Games in Berlin, Germany. During the actual games, the Alabama-born "Ebony Antelope" won four gold medals, set a new world's record, endured an insult from fascist dictator Adolf Hitler, and became an international superstar.

contributions to the nation's cultural history. One of these people, author Richard Wright (1908–1960), contributed by brilliantly depicting the inner thoughts and strivings of the black population's diverse segments. Born in Roxie, Mississippi, Wright grew up in grinding poverty, with reading and daydreaming his only escape from the bleakness of life. Deeply angered by the racial prejudice of the Deep South, he left Mississippi after completing the ninth grade, eventually landing in Chicago. Like many

other black men—even those with college degrees—
during the depression years, Wright worked in a series
of low-paying service jobs: dishwasher, delivery boy,
post office clerk. Even these positions were scarce, and
Wright spent part of his time in the 1930s looking for
work and standing in breadlines, waiting for free food
along with other hungry men and women. Frustrated,
angry, and despairing, he began listening to American
Communist party members, fiery speakers who denounced economic exploitation and racism. At this
time, the Communists were making a concentrated effort
to recruit blacks among both the urban poor and the
South's sharecroppers. Wright joined the party in
1932.

Wright remained a member of the Communist
party until 1942, when he resigned in disgust. The
Communists, he asserted, used the black cause more
than they served it, and they failed to make an active
protest against the persistent discrimination against
black Americans. (Wright recorded his Communist
party experiences in his autobiographical *American
Hunger*, written in 1945 but not published until 1977.)

Meanwhile Wright, who had known he was a
writer ever since his teenage years—at 15, he had
written his first short story, "The Voodoo of Hall's
Half Acre," which had been published in a black
weekly southern newspaper—continued to pour out
his feelings on paper. In 1936, a white mainstream
literary magazine published a Wright short story called
"Big Boy Leaves Home," which received unanimous
critical praise and started off his life as a professional
writer. His first book, a collection of short stories
entitled *Uncle Tom's Children*, appeared in 1938, and
in 1940, he published the novel most experts consider
his masterpiece: *Native Son*.

Set in Chicago, *Native Son* probes the racial tensions and violence that created such rebellious young
black men as the book's main character, Bigger

Gloria Madison and Richard Wright star in a 1950 film version of Wright's novel Native Son. *Published in 1940,* Native Son *stunned Americans with its gritty portrayal of a young man tragically warped by a racist society.*

Thomas. The novel became a Book-of-the-Month Club selection, virtually assuring Wright's future as a writer. In collaboration with white playwright Paul Green, Wright wrote the stage adaptation of *Native Son*, which opened on Broadway in 1941 with black actor Canada Lee (1907–1952) in the role of Bigger Thomas. The play proved a smash hit: "the biggest American drama of the season," said one important critic. Lee, too, received undiluted praise; the *New York Times* hailed his performance as "the most vital piece of acting on the current stage."

Two months before the stage premiere of *Native Son*, Wright had received the highest honor bestowed on black Americans: the NAACP's Spingarn Medal.

The award cited Wright for "his powerful depiction, in his works *Uncle Tom's Children* and *Native Son*, of the effects of discrimination and segregation and the denial of his rights as a citizen on the American Negro." But famous and respected as he was, Wright faced the same problems—in buying or renting houses, in being served in stores and restaurants, in being admitted to private clubs and houses—as every other black person in America, and by 1947, he had had his fill of it. Weary and disillusioned, he moved to France, where he would spent the remaining 13 years of his life.

Wright, who remains—possibly second only to W. E. B. Du Bois—the 20th century's most important black writer, went on to publish a sensational and hugely popular autobiography, *Black Boy*, in 1945. His subsequent work includes writings on his pilgrimage from the Deep South to the Middle West, from Chicago to New York, from the United States to Europe, Africa, and the East.

For black America, then, the depression years were more than a time of hardship, poverty, and trouble; these were years of amazing African American productivity in the worlds of drama, sports, and the arts. But black popular culture was not the only thing flourishing during the 1930s and 1940s; black political culture was entering a period of remarkable expansion and development as well.

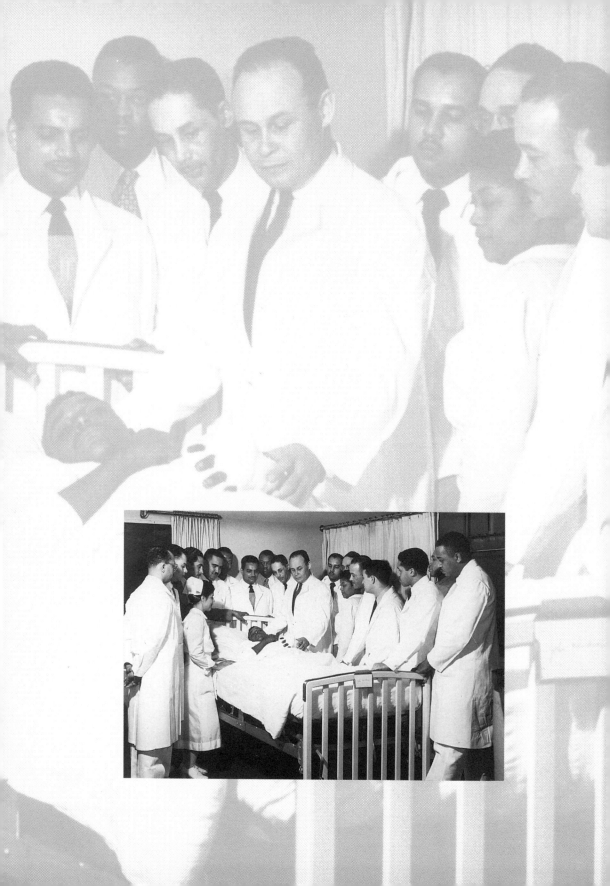

5

ORGANIZATIONS AND ATTITUDES

During the 1930s and 1940s, more African Americans obtained higher education than ever before—despite the fact that many schools were off-limits to them. At the end of World War I, only 3,000 African Americans were attending college, but by the beginning of World War II, approximately 45,000 were enrolled. The larger pool of educated black men and women resulted in more effective leadership, such as the bevy of talented black lawyers who spearheaded the NAACP's legal battle against discrimination.

Educated black Americans also attained prominence in the fields of medicine and science. One of the most outstanding physicians of the era was Charles Richard Drew. Born in 1904 in Washington, D.C., Drew attended Amherst College in Massachusetts, then McGill Medical College in Canada. During his internship at Montreal General Hospital, he began his pio-

Working at Freedmen's Hospital, the clinical facility of Howard University Medical College, in the early 1940s, Dr. Charles Drew (center, hands extended) treats a patient as interns look on. Drew developed both the medical and administrative techniques that made modern, large-scale blood banks possible.

neering work in blood research, investigating methods of storing and transporting blood for transfusions. Over the next few years, Drew discovered effective methods for preserving whole blood and pioneered the use of blood plasma (which could be dried and easily transported) as a substitute for whole blood. His work obtained him a spot on the Howard Medical College faculty in 1935 and a fellowship to Columbia University Medical School in 1938.

In 1940, Drew became head of the Blood for Britain project. The first large-scale blood bank, the organization collected blood in the United States, preserved it as plasma, and shipped it overseas. Drew proved an exceptional administrator, and in 1941, he became the assistant director of the American Red Cross blood procurement program. (There he opposed—to no avail—the Red Cross practice of segregating blood by race.) Drew's outstanding work in medicine resulted in his receipt of the NAACP's prestigious Spingarn Medal in 1944. Charles Drew died in 1950 as a result of injuries received in a car accident. (Contrary to popular legend, he was not refused treatment at a local hospital because of his race.) At Drew's funeral, Howard University president Mordecai Johnson praised his influential work, saying, "Here we have what rarely happens in history . . . a life which crowds into a handful of years significance so great men will never be able to forget it."

Blacks such as Charles Drew advanced science in the 1930s and 1940s. At the same time, mainstream science advanced in its attitudes toward black people.

Since the 1850s, pseudosciences such as craniometry (the measure of skulls as a means to determine intelligence) had been used to "prove" black inferiority. Not surprisingly, such theories were especially popular with white supremacists and fascists, who believed that such "evidence" of racial inferiority justified their poor treatment of black Americans and other minorities. For example, the late-19th-century craniometrist Gustave Le Bon was a strong influence on the Fascist Italian dictator Benito Mussolini, and Adolf Hitler subscribed to the theory that black people occupied some sort of halfway point on the evolutionary scale between apes and whites.

Mussolini and Hitler's boosting of what became known as scientific racism jarred American scientists into scrutinizing other supposed proofs of black inferiority. For example, during World War I, psychologist Robert M. Yerkes oversaw the intelligence quotient (IQ) testing of large numbers of army draftees. Yerkes concluded not only that blacks were less intelligent than whites, but that Jews, southern Europeans, and eastern Europeans were less intelligent than northern Europeans. His conclusions were widely accepted until 1945, when a new study of his data by psychologist Ashley Montagu demonstrated that the IQ tests actually measured the quality of the draftees' education. Yerkes's biases became evident when Montagu pointed out that, according to Yerkes's own data, the average black scores for the four northern states with the best public school systems exceeded the average white scores for the nine southern states. (Yerkes had already cast doubt on his own impartiality in 1941 by publicly praising the Fascists, claiming that "What has happened in [Nazi] Germany is the logical sequel to the psychological and personnel services in our own Army during 1917–18.")

Scholars in the social sciences also began to question their approach toward black people. For the most part, sociologists had neglected African American culture, and during the 1930s many of them came to realize how little they knew about black economic and social conditions. In 1935, the American Council on Education funded a major project for the study of African American youth. The project resulted in the 1940–41 publication by black scholars of five book-length studies that examined the situation of young African Americans from the rural South to the urban North.

An even larger project followed when the Carnegie Foundation moved to fund a comprehensive investigation of race relations in the United States. Deciding that an American researcher could never be unbiased on the subject, in 1937 the foundation offered a sizable grant to a Swedish social economist, Gunnar Myrdal. Myrdal assembled a research team that was a veritable *Who's Who* of up-and-coming black social scientists—including Charles S. Johnson, Allison Davis, E. Franklin Frazier, Ira De Agustine Reid, and Kenneth B. Clark—who researched and wrote reports on African American culture, religion, political organizations, and economic conditions. Myrdal also received input and aid from the NAACP, the National Urban League, and other black activist groups.

One of Myrdal's most important contacts at this time was Ralph Bunche, a black political science professor at Howard University. Bunche, born in Detroit, Michigan, in 1904, had graduated at the top of his class from the University of California at Los Angeles and had received master's and doctoral degrees from Harvard University. After joining Myrdal's staff in late 1938, he traveled with his chief across the South, interviewing scores of black and white southern-

Ralph Bunche studies a manuscript in the 1940s. A political science professor at Howard University, Bunche worked closely with Swedish social economist Gunnar Myrdal on Myrdal's ground-breaking 1944 book, An American Dilemma: The Negro Problem and Modern Democracy.

ers. He remained with the project until the research was completed in 1940, writing four lengthy reports on African American political leaders and organizations. Myrdal used the reports written by Bunche and the other researchers as the basis of his *An American Dilemma: The Negro Problem and Modern Democracy*, published in 1944.

The book, designed by Myrdal to be accessible to the general public as well as to academics, was a resounding success that would deeply influence the civil rights movement of the 1950s and 1960s. According to Myrdal biographer Walter A. Jackson in his *Gunnar Myrdal and America's Conscience: Social Engineering and Racial Liberalism, 1938–87* (1990):

> *An American Dilemma* . . . helped to create a new racial liberalism that influenced political leaders, judges, civil rights activists, and thousands of educated white

A Brotherhood of Sleeping Car Porters (BSCP) poster asserts that the organization "Stands For Service Not Servitude." The porters' attitude contrasted sharply with that of their employer, the Pullman Company, which hired only African Americans as porters because it believed blacks were naturally more servile than whites.

Americans. Myrdal's study was the key text in shaping a liberal orthodoxy in support of civil rights, desegregation, equal opportunity, and the assimilation of black citizens into mainstream American culture.

But books were hardly the only agents of change in the African American community, where working-class black people were making important inroads into the union movement. Black unionization got a boost when in 1935 John L. Lewis, a vice president of the American Federation of Labor (AFL)—which accepted racially segregated unions—left the federation. Lewis and his associates thereupon established the Committee for Industrial Organization (CIO), which forbade its member unions to exclude black workers; they even organized a political action committee to lobby for an end to racial discrimination in the workplace.

Despite its sanction of segregation, the AFL did contain integrated and all-black unions, most notably the Brotherhood of Sleeping Car Porters (BSCP). The brotherhood was also a sisterhood, representing the African American porters and maids who worked in the luxurious railroad cars of the Pullman Company;

it was headed by the prominent black labor leader A. Philip Randolph.

Born in Crescent City, Florida, in 1889 and a resident of Harlem, New York, after 1911, Randolph had never been a Pullman porter. Founder and editor of a militant black publication, the *Messenger*, he had gained a reputation as a fiery defender of black rights, and in 1925 representatives of the Pullman porters asked him to organize a union for them. The opposition of the Pullman Company made unionization of black railroad workers difficult, and because black employees could not join any of the established, whites-only railroad unions, Randolph had to build the brotherhood almost from scratch. A friend of Randolph's summed up the situation this way: "We thought Randolph was crazy. . . . [He was] going to fight Pullman's millions of dollars when half the time he didn't have a dime in his pocket."

The 1920s and early 1930s were lean years for the BSCP, but after the election of President Roosevelt in 1932, Congress passed a number of laws that helped strengthen organized labor and protect union organizers from employer reprisals. The Pullman Company

BSCP members gather in New York City for an 11th-anniversary parade in 1936, a year after the Roosevelt adminstration forced the Pullman Company to recognize the union.

was eventually forced to recognize and negotiate with the brotherhood in 1935.

Even the poorest black Americans organized during the 1930s and 1940s, most commonly in grassroots associations such as the Father Divine movement that mixed political agendas with spiritual elements. One of these organizations—a group that would rise to great prominence during the 1960s—was the Nation of Islam. The Nation was founded in 1930 in a Detroit, Michigan, ghetto known as Paradise Valley by a mysterious door-to-door peddler known variously as W. D. Fard, Master Farad Muhammad, or Wali Farad. Fard espoused a unique form of Islam that denounced whites as devils and advocated black separation—teachings that appealed to the desperately poor black residents of depression-era Detroit.

In 1934, after establishing a Temple of Islam

A federal marshal leads the handcuffed Elijah Muhammad to jail in 1942. Arrested on charges of inciting his followers to resist the wartime military draft, the 44-year-old Nation of Islam leader spent the next four years in prison.

in Detroit, Fard disappeared, and one of his disciples, Elijah Muhammad (born Elijah Poole, and renamed by Fard) took over leadership of the Detroit temple and established a second temple in Chicago. Although a comparatively small organization in the 1940s, the Nation attracted the attention of federal authorities during World War II when its members refused to serve in the armed forces. Muhammad was arrested in May 1942 on charges of inciting his followers to resist the draft, and he was held in a federal penitentiary in Milan, Michigan, until 1946.

Another organization that would regularly attract the attention of law-enforcement authorities was the American Communist party, which gained a substantial black membership during the 1930s. The party followed the directives of the Communist International, or Comintern, a worldwide Communist organization based in the Soviet capital, Moscow, and controlled by Soviet dictator Joseph Stalin. This connection with Moscow and Stalin caused serious alarm among U.S. government officials, and would ultimately prove the party's undoing.

In the early 1930s, the party began to focus its attention on the immediate problems facing black Americans, such as poor housing and job discrimination. The Communists showed remarkable skill at articulating the feelings of anger and discontent of dispossessed African Americans. The party soon began to attract black members, who were impressed by its strong line on racial equality and integration. Openly wooing black intellectuals, the party readily placed black party members in leadership positions. White Communists worked and lived in black neighborhoods; those who expressed racist sentiments were expelled from the party. Party branches in the South risked violence and persecution by holding illegal racially integrated meetings and attempting to organize a predominantly black union of sharecroppers.

The Communists also artfully exploited such outrages against blacks as the Scottsboro case, using these incidents as opportunities not only to promote their party as a defender of minority rights but also to mount vigorous attacks on other organizations working for civil rights, most notably the NAACP.

These efforts paid off as the American Communist party gained influence within black communities and among liberal whites. During the 1930s, such prominent blacks as actor and singer Paul Robeson, poet Langston Hughes, and scholar W. E. B. Du Bois made well-publicized trips to the Soviet Union, which they generally praised as a country without racial discrimination. Organizations with liberal or labor platforms such as the CIO, the Southern Conference for Human Welfare (an umbrella group of black and white liberal southern organizations), and the National Negro Congress (a civil rights organization that focused on labor issues, headed by A. Philip Randolph) readily accepted Communists as members. Communists who joined these organizations, however, often seemed more interested in taking over their leadership than in working with the non-Communist members.

The American Communist party became much more controversial in 1939, when Stalin signed a nonaggression pact with Adolf Hitler. The pact secretly divided up eastern Europe into two areas of influence, one to be dominated by Germany, the other by the Soviet Union. The world was shocked by the pact, whose true nature became evident when Germany invaded Poland, and the Soviet Union invaded Finland. U.S. Communists may well have been embarrassed or appalled by the pact, but party loyalty and discipline reigned supreme. The American Communist party stated their support for the pact, softened their attacks on Germany's Fascist regime, and backed pacifists in their attempts to keep the United States from entering World War II.

Battle lines were quickly drawn between non-Communist activists and Communists. The National Negro Congress, which by 1940 had been effectively taken over by Communists, passed a resolution affiliating the congress with an antiwar organization, triggering the immediate resignation of A. Philip Randolph as president. The animosity between Randolph and the Communists continued as he purged Communists from the Brotherhood of Sleeping Car Porters and resigned briefly from the Socialist party, which had adopted an antiwar stance. Randolph's attempt in 1941 to organize a march protesting discrimination in employment and the armed forces was bitterly opposed by the Communists because it was not an antiwar protest.

Black support for the Communists folded practically overnight. The Communists had vociferously attacked the NAACP in the 1930s, alienating supporters of that organization; now they were attacking the most prominent black labor leader in the country. Any remaining African American backing was lost after June 1941, when the American Communist party announced that the defense of the Soviet Union should take precedence over the fight for U.S. civil rights. Consequently, black activists who continued to press for equality were labeled as "fascist[s]" who were "sabotaging the war effort." By the end of the 1940s, even dedicated black Communists had left the party.

But there were to be further repercussions. In 1938, the House of Representatives established the House Un-American Activities Committee (HUAC), a unit responsible for investigating Fascist, Communist, and other radical organizations. Chaired by the ultraconservative Representative Martin Dies of Texas, HUAC quickly became a tool of the radical right wing, even charging Communist infiltration of President Roosevelt's New Deal programs. Civil rights activists soon came under scrutiny.

In 1943, HUAC charged distinguished educator and activist Mary McLeod Bethune with being a Communist worker for the Soviet Union. The committee based its accusation on two counts: McLeod's membership in the Southern Conference for Human Welfare and a speech she had made to the National Council on American-Soviet Friendship in which she had said: "I am deeply interested in the urgent needs of these people [the Soviets] and in having our people make some contribution in this area of world rehabilitation."

Because of Bethune's background, her friendship with the Roosevelts, and the extreme weakness of the evidence against her, her name was

Actor and singer Paul Robeson (left) greets scholar and activist W. E. B. Du Bois (right) at the 1949 World Peace Conference in Paris. Their interest in communism made both men targets of lengthy harassment campaigns by the U.S. government.

cleared within a month, but other prominent blacks fared less well at the hands of HUAC. Throughout the 1940s and 1950s, the committee targeted a number of notable African Americans—including Ralph Bunche, W. E. B. Du Bois, Langston Hughes, and Paul Robeson—who had displayed an interest in leftist politics or the Soviet Union or had joined organizations that also contained Communists. Some, like Bunche and Bethune, were readily exonerated, but others, such as Du Bois and Robeson, were harassed by the U.S. government for years on end.

Although the American Communist party and the Nation of Islam were subjects of government investigation during World War II, at that same time mainstream black organizations flourished, preparing the way for the successful civil rights crusades of the 1950s and 1960s. Even the smaller and more radical of these organizations had one important feature in common: they were usually begun by blacks and supported by everyday members of the black community. In the words of historian Geoffrey Perrett (in his *Days of Sadness, Years of Triumph: The American People, 1939–1945*, 1985), during the 1940s,

> the struggle for equality had finally struck out along the path of independent political action with the support of ordinary black people. A proving ground had been provided for a new corps of leaders and organizers. A new generation of young Negroes, college-educated and militant, was coming along to push even harder.

6

THE HOME FRONT

On September 1, 1939, Nazi Germany invaded Poland, using its superior weapons and armaments to overrun the country in a matter of days. Two days later, Great Britain and France declared war on Germany, and World War II had begun. The year 1940 saw Denmark, Norway, Belgium, the Netherlands, Luxembourg, and France fall to German military might.

Events in Europe shocked Americans. Now controlling a lion's share of the continent, Germany was opposed only by Great Britain, which was itself under constant threat of invasion. The sympathies of the American people lay firmly on the side of the British, but it was not clear to many people whether it would benefit the country to become directly involved in a long, bloody, European war. As a result, the United States did not send troops to aid Great Britain, instead adopting a program of aiding the British by lending them ships and other military supplies.

After World War I, America had all but disman-

Activists share a rare laugh during a 1940s labor demonstration. The picketers were protesting the refusal of many defense-industry plants to employ black workers.

tled its military, and it was obvious that the country was totally unprepared either to aid Great Britain or to wage war. Belated government recognition of this state of affairs resulted in one of the fastest military buildups of all time. The defense industry burgeoned as the government spent unprecedented amounts of money subsidizing new factories to produce the planes, ships, tanks, guns, and ammunition needed for a war effort. Defense-plant boomtowns sprang up overnight, and demand for both skilled and unskilled workers reached new highs, kicking the economy firmly out of its depression.

Initially, this boom all but passed African Americans by. According to an article in the August 1968 issue of *American Labor*,

> Building contractors begged for construction workers but 75,000 experienced Negro carpenters, painters, plasterers, cement workers, bricklayers and electricians could not get employment. It had been announced that 250,000 workers would be absorbed in supplying defense needs, but there was little place for Negro workers, regardless of training.
>
> The president of North American Aviation set forth the industry's thinking in a press interview, declaring that "regardless of training, we will not employ Negroes in the North American plant. It is against company policy."
>
> Standard Steel Corporation told the Kansas City Urban League: "We have not had a Negro worker in 25 years, and do not plan to start now."
>
> From the June 1942 issue of the Federal Security Agency publication: "Over 500,000 Negroes who should be utilized in war production are now idle because of the discriminatory hiring practices of war industries. Several million other Negroes engaged in unskilled occupations are prevented from making greater contributions."

Naturally, black activists objected to these policies, as they did to the military's policy of segregating black units and discriminating against black soldiers.

A number of meetings took place between President Franklin D. Roosevelt and prominent African American leaders, but the results were disappointing.

Labor leader A. Philip Randolph was especially displeased with the conferences. In December 1940, he and another labor activist, Milton Webster, were traveling on a train after yet another inconclusive meeting with Roosevelt. According to Randolph biographer Jervis Anderson (in his 1973 book, A. *Philip Randolph: A Biographical Portrait*), the two were sitting in silence when Randolph spoke up. "You know, Web," he said, "calling on the president and holding those conferences are not going to get us anywhere. We are going to have to do something about it." He paused. "I think we ought to get 10,000 Negroes to march on Washington in protest, march down Pennsylvania Avenue. What do you think of that?"

Webster replied somewhat cautiously that he thought it was a good idea. "But," he said, "where are you going to get 10,000 Negroes?"

"I think we can get them," was Randolph's only reply, and the two men lapsed back into silence. But Randolph was not silent long. He immediately began to organize the protest, which he called the March on Washington. The response from black Americans was so enthusiastic that Randolph began to plan for 100,000 marchers instead of 10,000. The notion of that many protesting black citizens descending on Washington, D.C., seemed at first preposterous to the Roosevelt administration, but when the president's wife, Eleanor Roosevelt, and a number of administration officials received invitations to speak at the march, it became obvious that Randolph was in earnest.

Hoping to persuade Randolph to cancel the march, the adminstration opened a series of negotiations with him. Randolph had one demand: the president must issue an executive order mandating nondiscrimination in hiring for both defense industry and govern-

Labor leader A. Philip Randolph (seen here in a portrait from the early 1930s) threatened to stage an enormous protest march in Washington, D.C., unless President Roosevelt agreed to condemn discriminatory hiring. Alarmed by the thought of such a demonstration during wartime, Roosevelt complied.

ment jobs, and the order had to "have teeth," meaning it must be enforceable. On June 25, 1941, six days before the scheduled date for the march, Roosevelt signed and issued Executive Order 8802, declaring "that there shall be no discrimination in the employment of workers in defense industries or government because of race, creed, color, or national origin," and establishing the Fair Employment Practices Committee (FEPC) to enforce this policy. Randolph called off the march. (Twenty-two years later Randolph would successfully resurrect the March on Washington, organizing 250,000 participants in the largest single protest demonstration in U.S. history.)

In obtaining Executive Order 8802, Randolph had in a sense lost the battle and won the war. His efforts demonstrated the effectiveness of the sort of mass-action pressure tactics that earlier, more conservative black leaders had avoided. His strategy, which forced the federal government to lead the way in the struggle for civil rights, would be copied with great effectiveness by civil rights activists (including Randolph himself) during the 1950s and 1960s.

The value of Randolph's approach was not immediately apparent because Executive Order 8802 triggered a furious backlash among white employers. Industries that had formerly hired black Americans began to adopt discriminatory hiring policies to counter what they saw as a growing militancy among African Americans. White supremacist organizations such as the Ku Klux Klan—whose membership was already growing at an unprecedented rate due to white fears of black soldiers—became all the more popular. Finally, the FEPC was crippled by its own machinery: the only way it could redress grievances was by canceling defense contracts, a move that would hamper defense production at a time when it was considered vital to national security. Consequently, the committee proved incapable of enforcing the new policy.

Randolph was unable to retaliate for the government's inaction by organizing another march; as the war drive gained momentum, the notion of disrupting the nation's leaders with a huge protest demonstration seemed all but treasonous to patriotic Americans of all races.

> Concerns about discrimination in employment went on the national back burner on December 7, 1941, when Japan launched a surprise attack on the U.S. naval base at Pearl Harbor, Hawaii. The United States promptly declared war on Japan, which was allied with Hitler's Germany and Mussolini's Italy. U.S. forces were soon fighting the Japanese in the Pacific, as well as German and Italian armies in North Africa and Europe. The defense industry's need for workers reached a new high just as the workforce was shrunk by the draft (the government's call to compulsory military service). Discriminatory policies or no, defense industries soon began hiring—and promoting—more and more black workers (although black women defense workers were still a rarity). The number of black Americans working in manufacturing jumped from 500,000 in 1940 to 1,200,000 in 1943—and 500,000 of these workers were organized into unions. The number of African American government employees increased fourfold in the years 1939–44.

Not many whites viewed these gains happily. A number of southern whites (and not a few northern ones) believed that the country—already endangered by the war—would become all the more vulnerable if black people got the upper hand. Many would have agreed with the mayor of Shreveport, Louisiana, who stated in the early 1940s: "Of equal importance to winning the war is the necessity of keeping Negroes out of skilled jobs." Racially inspired violence became increasingly common, much of it directed against black soldiers and factory workers.

Such violence particularly plagued the Michigan city of Detroit. Long the center of America's automobile industry, Detroit soon became capital of the defense manufacturing boom. New plants opened and wages increased, attracting nearly a half million workers, both white and black, to Detroit. Overcrowded housing became an increasingly acute problem, especially for black women and men, who were largely restricted to ghettos. Because of intense demand for the city's limited housing, black residents often paid double or triple the rent paid by whites. Although by 1943 black people constituted only 10 percent of Detroit's total population (and, because of ongoing discrimination, only 8.4 percent of the city's industrial job force), Detroit's black population had quadrupled from 1925 to 1943, alarming many whites and making the city a haven for white supremacist groups. By 1943, the Ku Klux Klan alone had 16,000 dues-paying members in Detroit. By the early 1940s, Detroit harbored a number of other hate groups as well.

Clearly, Detroit was a powder keg waiting to explode. The first spark landed in February 1942, when a number of black men and women attempted to move into the city's Sojourner Truth project, a federal housing development on the edge of a white neighborhood. When the black tenants tried to move in, hundreds of whites attacked them with stones and fists. In what would prove typical of its style, the all-white Detroit police force responded to the violence by using nightsticks, pistols, horses, and tear gas—against the black victims. Of the 20 people injured and 100 arrested that day, every one was black.

The situation in Detroit grew steadily tenser through the first half of 1943. White and black youths fought a number of street battles, at least one of which involved white soldiers stationed in Detroit. The Ku Klux Klan was directly involved in a series of automobile plant strikes, staged to protest the promotions of three black workers. Finally, at the end of one long, steamy 1943 day, Detroit's racial violence reached a brutal climax.

June 20 dawned hot. As temperatures soared above 90 degrees, tens of thousands of people, most of them black, poured into Belle Isle, an amusement park in the Detroit River. Near the island were both a naval base and the notorious black ghetto known as Paradise Valley. After a day of small-scale interracial fights between local blacks and white sailors, Belle Isle witnessed a wild, late-night free-for-all involving some 5,000 people.

Pursued by screaming whites, a lone black Detroiter (far right) runs for his life in June 1943. On the scene of the murder spree, the NAACP's Walter White reported one bright spot: he saw "many instances of Negroes defending their white neighbors and white neighbors protecting Negro friends."

Rumors spread quickly: Paradise Valley residents heard that whites had killed a black woman and her baby; people in white neighborhoods said a white woman had been raped and killed by black men. Black mobs began to attack passing whites and destroy white-owned businesses; gangs of whites did the same to black people. Anyone in the wrong place at the wrong time was a target. Soon gaining the upper hand, the white majority began dragging black people out of streetcars, movie theaters, and stores, then beating or shooting them. The NAACP's Walter White, who had raced to the beleaguered city at news of the riots, looked on in horror. Detroit's police officers, he noted with astonishment, simply "stood by and made no effort to check the assaults." Worse, many officers joined in attacks on black citizens.

The rioting raged all through the night and well into the next day, climaxing when a mob of 10,000 whites gathered at Paradise Valley and began hunting down black passersby. Finally federal troops arrived and, in the ultimate testimony to the incompetence of Detroit's police force, restored order within 30 minutes without firing a shot. After over 24 hours of uncontrolled rioting, the police had shot 17 blacks and no whites. Thirty-four people lay dead, more than 700 people were injured, and approximately $2 million worth of property had been destroyed.

Civic leaders in other urban areas rushed to defuse their own potential explosions. Nevertheless, race riots broke out that summer in El Paso and Port Arthur, Texas; in Springfield, Massachusetts; in Hubbard, Ohio; and in Los Angeles, California, where a particularly violent series of attacks on Mexican Americans by white soldiers and policemen took place. The largest race riot involving African Americans took place in Harlem, New York, less than two months after the Detroit unrest.

Harlem was no stranger to discord. In 1935, a

minor incident involving the arrest of a shoplifter sparked a brief yet violent riot that left three people dead. Like Detroit, New York had experienced a population explosion during the early 1940s, resulting in a housing shortage that was especially severe in black neighborhoods. But while black residents in both New York and Detroit had to pay more for housing, Harlemites had the extra burden of having to pay more for food. Food prices were regulated by the Office of Price Administration to prevent wartime profiteering (the making of excessive profits), but in Harlem, price controls were rarely enforced, and white-owned grocery stores charged considerably more for food there than in white neighborhoods. In addition, many a son of Harlem had enlisted or been drafted into the U.S. military, and reports of routine mistreatment and violence directed against black soldiers stationed in southern military bases had enraged the community.

On August 1, 1943, a black soldier, Private Robert Bandy, and his mother were checking out of a Harlem hotel as a black woman who was trying to get a refund became very disorderly. The hotel clerk called in a policeman, white officer James Collins, who started pushing the woman out of the hotel. Believing that Collins was treating her with unnecessary roughness, Bandy confronted him, and the two began to fight. Bandy's mother soon joined in the fight, which ended when Bandy seized Collins's nightstick and Collins shot Bandy in the shoulder. The wound was not serious, but the repercussions of the fight would be.

To Harlemites, the fight between Bandy and Collins seemed to represent all the abuse black soldiers and civilians had been taking at the hands of white authority. An angry crowd attacked Collins, and rumors quickly spread throughout Harlem that a black soldier, attempting to defend his mother, had been shot and killed by a white policeman. Soon, furious black residents were smashing windows of white-owned shops, followed by crowds of looters.

The integrated New York police force proved far more effective at curtailing violence than its Detroit counterpart, and the mayor of New York, Fiorello La Guardia, used black volunteers, civilian groups, and labor organizations to restore peace. Walter White maintained in a report on the Harlem riot that in Detroit "the Mayor was weak and the police inefficient. Neither condition prevails here." And black minister and city councilman Adam Clayton Powell, Jr., characterized La Guardia's handling of the riot as "wise and effective." In Detroit, civic officials did everything in their power to block an investigation of the causes of the riot, preferring to blame the city's black citizens, the black press, and the NAACP for the violence (this last accusation was withdrawn when the association's lawyers threatened the mayor of Detroit with a libel suit). In New York, on the other hand, officials welcomed investigations by such independent organizations as the NAACP, the CIO, and an association of Harlem store owners. In response to the recommendations made by these investigations, Mayor La Guardia promised to improve Harlem's housing conditions, funded programs to combat juvenile delinquency, and cracked down on stores that were violating price controls.

Property damage in Harlem was extensive: 1,450 stores were destroyed and $5 million worth of property was damaged. Casualties, however, were fewer than in the Detroit riot: 6 people were killed (4 of them by police) and 543 injured. Unlike the Detroit riot, the turmoil in Harlem did not turn into an all-out race war between ordinary blacks and whites. It had, instead, as historian Alfred McClung Lee has said in his *Race Riot: A First Hand Observation of the 1943 Detroit Riots* (1967), "the character of [an] uprising against police and merchants as symbols of white

domination." Preferred targets for rioters were white-owned grocery stores and pawnshops, both potent symbols of white financial exploitation. White policemen were also targeted by rioters, and 53 of them were injured. In many ways, the Detroit riots harked back to the race wars that had rocked the country after World War I, while the Harlem riot pointed toward things to come. The urban riots of the 1960s and the Los Angeles riot of 1992 would be what Lee calls "riots of desperation," fueled more by the frustrations of poverty and ghettoization than by pure race hatred.

The 1943 riots made clear the devastating cost of racial tension in the United States. The fact that the only areas of calm during the Detroit riots were the rare neighborhoods and factories that were racially integrated was not lost on observers. Integrated organizations dedicated to promoting good race relations began to crop up throughout the United States; among them were the Southern Regional Council and

An automobile burns during the Harlem riot of August 1943. Unlike the Detroit melee, the New York disturbance was less about race than about money; tired of being poor in the midst of plenty, Harlem mobs attacked property, not people.

Harlem residents inspect a local store the morning after the 1943 riot. The shop's quick-thinking manager had carefully posted his racial identity, thereby deflecting looters intent on wrecking white-owned businesses.

the American Council on Race Relations in the Midwest. A group founded in 1943 by black and white pacifists and calling itself the Congress of Racial Equality (better known as CORE) gained sufficient strength to organize its first protest campaign against racism, the Summer Non-Violent Direct Action Campaign to Help Uproot Jim Crowism in an American Community, in 1945. And the NAACP did even better, growing from 50,000 members and 355 branches in 1940 to 500,000 members and 1,000 branches by the end of the war.

Some progress was made even in the traditional bastions of segregation: the American Bar Association admitted its first African American member in 1943, and in 1944 a black journalist was admitted to presidential press conferences for the first time. But the most dramatic incident occurred when, in 1943, the Daughters of the American Revolution invited contralto Marian Anderson to sing for a war-relief benefit held in

Washington's Constitution Hall, the very spot that the organization had barred her from using only four years before.

Even the FEPC seemed to redeem itself when in 1944 it forced the city of Philadelphia to promote eight black workers to the position of streetcar drivers. Protesting the move, white streetcar drivers struck for five days, paralyzing the city and bringing racial tensions to new highs, but the federal government stood its ground, eventually sending in troops to break the strike. To avoid such confrontations in the future, Philadelphia quietly opened up more and more jobs to black residents. In an indication of the new popularity of both the FEPC and nondiscriminatory hiring, 20 states created state committees similar to the FEPC when it seemed likely that the federal committee would be dissolved at the end of the war.

Discrimination against African Americans in hiring was still commonplace, but by the end of World War II, the tide was beginning to turn in favor of American blacks. The federal government had, for the first time, announced and enforced a policy of nondiscrimination in hiring. More important, the federal government had done so at the behest of a powerful black organization. Blacks were organizing into labor unions and civil rights groups in unprecedented numbers as more and more ordinary African Americans were discovering that they, too, could create change.

7

SERVICE TO ONE'S COUNTRY

Given Hitler's racial theories and Mussolini's invasion of Ethiopia, it is not surprising that many African Americans were highly supportive of the war effort. Although a number of black organizations strongly opposed both the war and the involvement of African Americans in the war effort, these groups were quite small. The majority of African Americans believed that blacks should fight for the United States, even though they were denied many of the basic rights and privileges of citizens.

The U.S. armed forces, however, were considerably less eager to accept black soldiers. Although black men had served with distinction in the military since the American Revolution, the virulent racism that swept the country during and after World War I left its mark on the armed forces. The navy accepted black men only as mess attendants (food servers), the army generally assigned them to service rather than combat duty, and the Army Air Corps (the precursor to today's air force) and the marines excluded black men entirely. As a result of such policies, at the war's

Mechanic Marjorie Dorsey chats with air force cadet Cornelius Rogers as she repairs a fighter plane at the Army Air Force Training Center in Tuskegee, Alabama, in 1943. Although the Army Air Force accepted blacks soon after the war began, it kept them strictly segregated throughout the conflict.

beginning fewer than 4,000 black soldiers—less than 2 percent of the troops—served in the U.S. Army. And only five army officers, three of them chaplains, were African Americans.

Black soldiers served in segregated units (often commanded by white officers), and black officers could not command white troops. In 1938 the army instituted a policy decreeing that the proportion of black Americans in the military could not exceed the proportion of blacks in the country as a whole. (No such policy existed for any other ethnic or racial group.) As black Americans made up approximately 10 percent of the U.S. population at the time, no more than 10 percent of U.S. troops could be black (although, due to discriminatory draft policies, the percentage of black Americans in the armed forces during World War II never exceeded 8 percent).

As early as 1939, black activists were attempting to persuade Congress and the White House to eliminate these racial barriers. Hoping to open the Army Air Corps to black men, the NAACP lobbied for the establishment of black civilian flight-training schools, and in the fall of the year civilian pilot-training units opened at a number of black colleges. In 1940 educator and activist Mary McLeod Bethune began a series of meetings with Eleanor Roosevelt concerning discrimination in the armed forces; the two women's talks led to a number of high-level conferences between White House officials and prominent African American activists. "V for Victory," a popular wartime slogan, was quickly modified by black newspapers into "Double V"—victory over the forces of fascism abroad and the forces of racism at home. (Indeed, the black press was so thorough in its coverage of racism on the home front during the war that the Justice Department considered indicting a number of black newspaper editors on charges of sedition and interference with the war effort.)

Black activism increased when Congress passed the Selective Training and Service Act of 1940. This law established a peacetime draft in order to ensure an adequate number of trained troops in case the country went to war. The result of tireless lobbying by black activists, the law contained an antidiscrimination clause stating "any person, regardless of race or color, . . . shall be afforded an opportunity to volunteer for induction into the land or naval forces of the United States." The clause, however, did not address segregation within the service, nor did it condemn the military's practice of rarely training black men for combat or allowing them into battle. To make things worse, a policy statement released by the White House in October upheld segregation in the armed forces—and falsely implied that a number of black leaders supported the practice as well.

Demanding an end to military segregation—still practiced by the U.S. armed forces three years after the end of World War II—A. Philip Randolph (left) leads a 1948 protest march outside the Democratic National Convention headquarters in Philadelphia.

The resulting furor prompted the army to promote its highest-ranking African American, Colonel Benjamin O. Davis, Sr., to the rank of brigadier general, making him the first black general in the United States since Reconstruction. Davis was a career soldier who had served the army since the turn of the century. Although black leaders agreed that he strongly deserved the honor, its timing (just over a week before the 1940 presidential election and a mere eight months before Davis's scheduled retirement) made it look like a mere political ploy, effected only to keep black voters loyal to the Roosevelt ticket.

General Davis, however, put off his retirement until after the war and easily put an end to fears that he would serve merely as window dressing for an unreformedly racist military. Instead, he became a valuable staff member of the inspector general's office and the army's Advisory Committee on Negro Troop Policies, reporting racial incidents and promoting more equitable treatment of black soldiers.

Although the efforts of such individuals as Davis would eventually improve the lot of African American soldiers and sailors, the armed forces initially demonstrated a good deal of hostility to black enlistees. Military racial discrimination usually started with local draft boards, which often inducted whites ahead of blacks. Even when draft boards did not practice racial discrimination, blacks were less likely to be inducted than whites because of the high rates of disease, malnutrition, and illiteracy that plagued the black population—the result of the severe poverty

Brigadier General Benjamin O. Davis, Sr., attends a War Department press conference in 1943 with his son, Lieutenant Colonel Benjamin O. Davis, Jr. Both men—the father a 44-year army veteran, and the son a much-decorated fighter pilot—had become national heroes through their war service and dedication to civil rights.

of the Great Depression. Healthy African Americans got around racist draft boards by volunteering for service; from 1940 to 1941 black men made up slightly more than 16 percent of the army's volunteers.

For African American soldiers and sailors, getting into the armed forces proved only the first hurdle in what was often a deeply frustrating experience. Officer candidates trained together regardless of race, but training units for enlisted black men were strictly segregated until 1943. Black units could not use the same mess halls or recreational facilities as the white units, and those facilities set aside for blacks were commonly inadequate and inferior. During World War II, more than 50 percent of the military's officers

Black GIs hammer out the war in a military shoe-repair shop in the South Pacific. The African American soldiers allowed to see action usually performed with valor, but the armed forces stubbornly kept most blacks in noncombat positions.

came from the Deep South; according to one black soldier, these officers "had no compunctions about calling us 'niggahs,' and to them 'boy' was almost a term of praise." In addition, many military bases were situated in the Deep South. Outside the bases, black soldiers were expected to defer to white people in every way—and sometimes paid with their lives if they did not.

This sort of treatment came as a shock to northern black men; in one case a large group of black soldiers stationed in a southern army base deserted and returned to their former post in Michigan. Racist white civilians and soldiers were no more pleased by the large number of armed, assertive black men that had appeared in their communities seemingly overnight. Racial violence became almost commonplace, beginning with the apparent lynching of a black private by white soldiers in the spring of 1941 at Fort Benning, Georgia (army officials dismissed the incident as a suicide), and continuing throughout the year.

But in 1941 the news for black men in the army was not all bad. The prestigious Army Air Corps announced in March that it would accept African American applicants for aviation cadet training and—true to the Jim Crow policy of the regular army—proceeded to construct an airfield at Tuskegee University in Alabama for the separate training of black cadets. In July 1941, the first group of cadets (including the son of General Davis, West Point graduate Benjamin O. Davis, Jr.) began training, forming the nucleus of the all-black 99th Pursuit Squadron. The well-publicized combat successes of the 99th, which later expanded into the 332nd Fighter Group, would help lay to rest the notion that black Americans were unwilling to risk their lives for their country.

But in 1941 the most visible black fighter was not a glamorous air force pilot; he was a navy mess attendant. Dorie Miller, son of Texas sharecroppers, enlisted in the navy in 1938 and was later assigned to the battleship *Arizona*, stationed at Pearl Harbor, Hawaii. When the Japanese air force attacked the naval base on December 7, 1941, the 22-year-old Miller was below decks in relative safety. But his captain, on deck and exposed to enemy fire, was seriously wounded. A pharmacist's mate asked the brawny Miller (at the time the heavyweight boxing champion of the *Arizona*) to help him move the captain to a more protected area of the deck. Miller readily obliged, exposing himself to enemy fire in an attempt to save the captain.

While treating the captain's wounds (which proved fatal), the mate noticed that Miller had disappeared. Recounting the incident later, the mate said he then spotted Miller manning a machine gun, "blazing away as though he had fired one all his life." The regular gunner had been killed by the bullets and shrapnel still pouring onto the ship, and the mess attendant had courageously stepped in to continue his shipmate's work. Miller shot down at least two and perhaps as many as six enemy aircraft before running out of ammunition and being ordered off the deck. On May 27, 1942, the navy cited Miller for his "distinguished devotion to duty, extraordinary courage and disregard for his own personal safety" and awarded him a Navy Cross. In November of the next year the decorated mess attendant went down with the *Lipscomb Bay* in the South Pacific, but in his short lifetime he had, in the words of historian Geoffrey Perrett, "made mockery of the premise on which the navy accepted Negroes only as mess attendants."

In 1942 the navy, under considerable pressure from President Roosevelt, began to loosen restrictions on black volunteers, allowing African Americans to enlist in previously segregated units and to obtain positions other than that of mess attendant. Black men who were not mess attendants were not allowed on the high seas, however, and many blacks were delegated menial duties such as loading ships. That same year the marines also began to admit African American volunteers, creating an all-black battalion at Camp Lejeune in North Carolina. Literally forced by the Roosevelt administration to accept blacks, the

Admiral Chester Nimitz awards the Navy Cross to messman Dorie Miller, one of America's first World War II heroes. Serving on the USS Arizona during the 1941 Japanese attack on Pearl Harbor, Hawaii, Miller had seized a fallen gunner's weapon and shot down as many as six enemy aircraft. Decorated but never promoted, Miller was killed in action in 1943.

marines earned a reputation for making them feel unwelcome. Bill Downey, one of the first black marines, recalls in his memoir *Uncle Sam Must Be . . . Losing the War: Black Marines of the 51st* (1982),

> Colonel Samuel A. Woods, Jr., a southerner in the old tradition and a true-blue Marine himself, had been chosen as the first commanding officer. The old colonel tried to be diplomatic about his feelings of white superiority. He continually told us, "his boys," that he understood if we couldn't measure up.

The decision to admit black men was so poorly publicized that when one battalionmate of Downey's went to his Alabama hometown on leave, the local sheriff arrested him for impersonating a marine.

But these discouraging incidents were trifles com-

A black platoon from the 104th Division takes a breather in the German town of Scherfede, where, in April 1945, they had just captured an entire unit of Nazi storm troopers. U.S. forces were never fully integrated during World War II, but the awesome performance of black combat troops paved the way for change.

pared to the standard military policy of using black troops primarily as domestic service units. The military sent a considerably smaller percentage of black troops overseas than white troops, using the blacks to replace white service troops, who would then be reassigned to the coveted combat positions. Black units were often trained for combat, then converted by the military into service units—a humiliating bait and switch for black men eager to fight. In his memoirs, Downey remembers the "general anger and resentment for being hoodwinked into thinking we would someday be a crack combat Marine force," and quotes one of his battalionmates as exclaiming, "If I wanted to be a . . . waiter, I wouldn't have joined the Marine Corps, I'd have joined the Waldorf-Astoria Hotel!"

The policy created headaches for the military command as well. Low morale resulted in an increase in racial violence on military bases in 1943 and 1944. Unlike the incidents in 1941, these clashes were just as likely to be started by angry and disaffected black troops as by racist whites.

Black units that did engage in combat had their performance scrutinized in a way that white units did not. For example, when the Army Air Corps's all-black 99th Pursuit Squadron (later the 332nd Fighter Group) first fought, in North Africa in April 1943, the inexperienced squadron did not perform especially well. Official reports suggested that the unit was inferior to similar white units. By October, a review of all the black army units in combat indicated that black soldiers were inferior to whites in combat, and recommended that black air units no longer be used on the front. Despite a report by General Dwight D. Eisenhower praising the 99th squadron and suggesting that black troops had not been adequately tested in battle to support any conclusions about their performance, the drive to remove black men from combat gained momentum in the military and was stopped only by intense political and public pressure applied to military officials in the United States. Ironically, by the end of the war the pilots of the 332nd Fighter Group were some of the most highly decorated in the force, and the group as a whole received a presidential citation for their outstanding work in North Africa and Europe.

By December 1944, the Allied forces, led by the United States, had taken Rome and were driving the German forces out of France toward the German capital of Berlin. On December 16, Germany suddenly struck back with a last-ditch surprise assault on Allied lines that would be known as the Battle of the Bulge. Suffering heavy initial losses, the U.S. Army desperately needed more combat troops, especially infantry riflemen. As a result, high army officials sent out a letter to black service troops that read in part:

> The Commanding General . . . is happy to offer to a limited number of colored troops who have had infantry training, the privilege of joining our veteran units at the front to deliver the knockout blow. . . . Your comrades at the front

are anxious to share the glory of victory with you. Your relatives and friends everywhere have been urging that you be granted this privilege.

Not only would African Americans be given the opportunity to fight, the letter said, but "it is planned to assign [black troops] without regard to color or race to units where assistance is most needed."

Black soldiers rushed to volunteer. In some units far from the front, as many as 8 in 10 men applied; in one engineer unit, 171 of the 186 men applied. In order to keep the service units from losing all their men, army officials quickly limited the offer to 2,500 volunteers, turning down almost 3,000 additional applicants.

The offer almost disappeared as soon as it materialized. When the War Department in Washington, D.C., got wind of the offer, it immediately demanded that the plan be scrapped. The need for combat troops was great, however, and a compromise plan was reached. Black troops were not completely integrated into white units; instead black platoons fought side by side with white platoons. Although the new plan was something of a disappointment, morale radically improved among African American soldiers. Reporting from the scene, Walter White observed,

> Of all the Negroes who were thus permitted to fight, only two went AWOL [absent without leave]. Their platoon had not at the time seen action because it was stationed in the rear as reserve troops. The whereabouts of the two deserters was discovered a few days after their disappearance when a frontline division commander reported that the two Negroes had "reported to him to fight!"

To the surprise of many military "experts," white and black combat troops worked well together, with little or none of the racial friction that had plagued the segregated U.S. military

bases. An army report quoted one white sergeant from South Carolina who had fought with black soldiers in an infantry unit as saying, "When I heard about it, I said I'd be damned if I'd wear the same shoulder patch they did. After that first day, when we saw how they fought, I changed my mind." Black infantry troops formed an essential part of the Allied military drive across Germany that forced Germany's surrender on May 7, 1945, thus ending the war in Europe.

African American servicemen shone not only in the European theater but in the Pacific as well. Especially notable was the performance of black marines in one of the key Pacific battles, the struggle for the island of Iwo Jima. An ideal base for Japan-bound aircraft, the island was also large enough to provide landing space for the air corps's huge B-29 bombers. The Japanese, keenly aware of Iwo Jima's strategic importance, were ready to defend it with some 21,000 soldiers equipped with mortars, machine guns, and antitank weapons. On February 19, 1945, 80,000 marines launched an invasion of the island that was to last more than a month and include some of the fiercest combat of the war.

According to marine policy, black troops could perform only service duties, but, according to Perrett, "the corps was so combat-oriented that it absentmindedly started to ignore its own policy." Iwo Jima proved the point: five days after the initial landing and in the midst of ferocious fighting, four companies of black marines were assembled as the 8th Field Depot to supply the invading troops with ammunition and supplies. This so-called service duty involved landing in rough seas on wreckage-strewn beaches, braving heavy enemy fire, and moving supplies through sand too loose to allow the use of motor vehicles. The men of the 8th Field Depot delivered their supplies, then dug in to help battle the enemy.

The marines' casual disregard of its own "black policy" led to a formal change in its treatment of blacks: a few months after the August 1945 Japanese surrender, the proud corps reversed a long-standing policy and commissioned its first African American officer.

The change in the marines' race policy originated in battle, but change in naval policy came from the top down. In 1944, when James V. Forrestal, a long-time member of the National Urban League, became secretary of the navy, he began an active program of encouraging racial equality. Soon after he took office, he eliminated the policy that banned sea duty to all black men except mess stewards. Forrestal then ordered the manning of two small vessels with all-black crews. Most of the officers on both ships were white, but the navy announced its intention to replace them with black officers as soon as the blacks' training was complete. Finally, on February 27, 1946, the navy removed all restrictions on black personnel and prohibited racial segregation in naval housing and facilities. In only a few years, the navy had gone from being a bastion of racial discrimination to being the only racially integrated branch of the military.

A number of black women also served in World War II, although in considerably smaller numbers than black men. Sixty-five-hundred African American women served in the Women's Army Auxiliary Corps (known after September 1943 as the Women's Army Corps, or WAC), 146 of them as officers. Created in May 1942, the WAC gave its members appropriate training to perform service tasks in the armed forces, thus freeing male soldiers for combat duties. The WAC was organized along the lines of the army, and as a result, it too maintained a quota of 10 percent black membership. The women's corps also officially followed a policy of strict racial segregation—a policy that initially made the service branch remarkably unpopular with young black women. As a result, Mary McLeod Bethune, acting as an unofficial adviser to the War Department, had to make several public pleas for members before enough black applicants could be found to fill the quota.

Although the WAC segregated African American women, it also offered them a policy of nondiscrimination in service assignments. Unlike the regular army, the WAC allowed black officers to command white enlistees, and promised them equal access to officers' training school and technical schools. Nondiscrimination, however, proved easier to promise than to practice. In 1945, four African American WACs working as orderlies at Lovell General Hospital at Fort Devens, Massachusetts, were courtmartialed and sentenced to one year's hard labor and dishonorable discharge from the service for refusing to report for duty. The women had gone on strike to protest their treatment by their commandant, a white noncommissioned officer. In defiance of War Department policy, he had assigned all black WACs to orderly duty and had reportedly exclaimed, "I don't want any black WACs as medical technicians around this hospital. I want them to scrub and do the dirty work." The verdict was finally overturned and the commandant removed from his post by the War Department, but the experience was an emotionally harrowing one for the women involved. (African American soldiers and sailors who were deemed too militant by their commanding officers were also frequently court-martialed on trumped-up charges.)

After a lengthy struggle, black women also served in the armed forces as nurses. African American nurses had served in the Army Nurse Corps only in token numbers during World War I, and by the time of the Japanese attack on Pearl Harbor, there were no black nurses in any branch of the armed forces. The National Association of Colored Graduate Nurses (NACGN), led by Mabel Staupers (who won the 1951 Spingarn Medal for her efforts to integrate nursing), encouraged its members to enroll in the American Red Cross, which was then acting as a medical-staff procurement agency for the military. The Red Cross readily accepted the nurses, but the military did not. Both the Army and the Navy Nurse Corps declared in 1941 that they would accept no black nurses, a position the Army Nurse Corps grudgingly reversed later that year when it announced that it would accept 56 black nurses who were to serve only in segregated hospitals or wards, tending only to black soldiers.

Enraged, NACGN activists launched an extensive media campaign to eliminate the quota. In the meantime, large numbers of white nurses went off to war, creating a civilian nurse shortage that opened unprecedented employment opportunities for black nurses. In addition, the Cadet Nurse Corps was created to subsidize the education of nurses, and many African American women were suddenly able to afford nursing school. The number of black nursing students skyrocketed, and by 1945 about 2,600 African Americans were enrolled in nursing school, a 135 percent increase over the number enrolled in 1939.

In 1943, the army raised its quota of black nurses to 160. Half of the African American nurses in the army at this time were assigned to Fort Huachuca, Arizona, under the direction of Lieutenant Susan Elizabeth Freeman. Freeman, who had studied nursing at the Freedmen's Hospital School of Nursing, Howard University, and Columbia University, had joined the Army

Nurse Corps in 1941 and been assigned to Camp Livingston, Louisiana. Freeman was the first nurse at the camp, black or white, to receive a promotion to first lieutenant; as a result, according to *Crisis* editor Roy Wilkins, "a 'situation' existed for a few days until the promotion of a white nurse came through." Freeman continued to prove an exceptional leader and nurse, leaving Fort Huachuca in 1943 to serve in Liberia as chief nurse of the first overseas unit of African American nurses. During this time, she and eight other nurses received a unit commendation from the Office of the Commanding General, and Freeman herself was made a knight official of the Liberian Humane Order of Africa Redemption by the Liberian government.

Not all black nurses stationed overseas were so well treated. Black army nurses stationed in England were allowed to attend only German prisoners of war, a situation the nurses found offensive and humiliating. Staupers met with Eleanor Roosevelt in November 1944 to protest this practice, telling the president's wife that when African American nurses join the army "it is with the high hopes that they will be used to nurse sick and wounded soldiers who are fighting our country's enemies and not primarily to care for these enemies." The restriction was eventually lifted.

Finally, on January 20, 1945, the Army Nurse Corps agreed to accept nurses without regard to race and was promptly swamped with African American volunteers. According to historian M. Elizabeth Carnegie in her 1988 book, *The Path We Tread*, "the number of Negro nurses who volunteered and were commissioned in the last year of the war almost equalled the total in the army in September 1944."

A New York Amsterdam News *cartoon, entitled "Glad to see you . . . Now," mocks the Army Nurse Corps's belated decision to accept black volunteers. Although it was desperately short of nurses, the corps maintained its whites-only policy until January 1945, seven months before Japan's surrender ended the war.*

Eleven days after the army's announcement, the navy released a statement that read in part, "there is no policy in the Navy which discriminates against the utilization of Negro Nurses."

During World War II, more than 700,000 black men served in the army, 165,000 in the navy, 17,000 in the marines, and 5,000 in the integrated Coast Guard. More than 4,000 black women served in the army and navy's women's corps, and some 500 served as military nurses. More than 500,000 black Americans had served overseas, where they were often treated better by the local people than by their fellow soldiers.

Black veterans were sometimes targeted for violence by white racists, but the end of World War II did not see the large-scale riots and lynchings that had followed World War I. Most important, black veterans were eligible for equal benefits under the G. I. Bill, which provided World War II veterans with federal funding to buy a home, start a business, finish high school, attend college, learn a trade, or get a government job. In addition, the Veterans' Administration pledged not to discriminate against blacks, granting black veterans equal access to subsidized medical care.

Black veterans returned from service to a country that was in the midst of a major economic upswing. They could attend college on the G. I. Bill (as 250,000 ultimately did), receive high-quality medical care, or use the technical skills they had learned in their military training to get jobs or start businesses. But most important, black veterans had seen political pressure and individual acts of heroism provoke meaningful changes in the racial policy of one of the most conservative institutions in the country, the U.S. military. After World War I, the legal and economic situation of blacks improved but little. After World War II, African Americans were determined that the political and social gains made during the war would increase.

8

AFTER THE WAR

Although African Americans still had formidable barriers to overcome in the quest for equality, postwar America offered hope as well as anxiety. The defense industry laid off many workers, bringing fears that the high unemployment of the 1930s would return, but a boom in civilian industries took up much of the slack. Many unions were now integrated, giving added job security to African American workers. The federal government maintained its policy of nondiscrimination in government hiring, creating a whole new market for black women and men seeking employment. Even African American women, who had been for the most part excluded from both the armed forces and defense-industry jobs, had begun to move out of low-paying jobs as maids and servants and into new fields such as clerical work, which had experienced severe labor shortages during the war. Many African Americans had obtained valuable work skills during the war through additional training and education on the job, military service, or subsidized college programs.

Members of the integrated American Federation of State, County, and Municipal Employees in St. Louis, Missouri, vote on a local issue in 1954. The postwar opening of labor unions to blacks assisted them in getting higher wages, greater employment opportunities, and more job security.

Many African Americans also benefited from the federal social programs created during the war. In 1941, fully half of all draftees were rejected for service due to health problems caused primarily by malnutrition—a situation that appalled federal officials and spurred them to expand the New Deal's food-stamp and school-lunch programs. The defense-plant boomtowns that sprang up around the country during the war had lacked both adequate housing and medical facilities, alarming federal officials, who feared that diseases would spread among defense workers and worsen the labor shortage. To ward off this threat, the federal government built subsidized housing and opened free medical clinics for the workers, giving many poor African Americans their first access to decent homes and proper health care. As a result of efforts to improve public health and the wartime increase in income, from 1939 to 1945 the life span of African Americans increased five years—despite the fact that a major war with sizable casualties occurred at the time.

The "Double V" strategy had also led to improvements in the field of civil rights, especially voting rights. The most notable victory in this field was the elimination of the so-called white primary in the South. Because of the Reconstruction activities of the Radical Republicans, the only candidates who could reasonably expect to win an election in the South were members of the Democratic party. Consequently, the Democratic primary election, held to determine who would become the Democratic party's candidate for office, took on the importance of a final election. In order to keep African Americans from exercising their right to vote, southern state legislatures passed laws excluding black citizens from voting in party primaries. The Supreme Court declared unconstitutional such "white primaries" as early as 1927, but during the 1930s and 1940s, state

An effigy presents a grim warning to would-be African American voters. By the late 1940s, after fighting a long, dangerous battle to defeat southern restrictions on the black franchise, the NAACP had scored enough Supreme Court victories to ensure the voting rights of all Americans, black and white alike.

legislatures instituted a variety of laws that indirectly (but effectively) excluded African Americans from primaries.

The Texas state legislature was especially creative in this regard. After the 1927 ruling, the governor of Texas called a special session of the state legislature to pass a new law: the resulting legislation allowed the Democratic party's state executive committee to draw up its own rules concerning who could vote in its primaries, rather than empowering the state legislature to do so. The party committee promptly declared that no black Texans could vote in Democratic primary elections. The NAACP challenged the actions of the state legislature before the Supreme Court in 1932. The Court found that the Texas law had the effect of excluding black residents from voting and was thus unconstitutional.

Texas tried again. The Democratic state convention, without any explicit encouragement from the legislature, voted to exclude African Americans from primary elections. The NAACP challenged the action and took the case, *Grovey v. Townsend*, all the way up to the Supreme Court in 1935—and lost. The Court held that a political party was a private organization, and thus could include or exclude whomever it wished from participating in its activities.

Southern states now had a constitutional means to exclude African Americans from voting—a serious blow to civil rights. Thurgood Marshall, who became director-counsel for the NAACP Legal Defense and Education Fund in 1940, decided that the Fund would have to tackle the white primary head-on. In 1941 a Houston doctor, Lonnie E. Smith, filed suit against the Texas Democratic party for preventing him from voting in a primary the previous year. The case was dismissed by the lower courts, and in 1944 Marshall took the case before the Supreme Court. Marshall was seeking nothing less than the overruling of *Grovey v. Townsend*—and he got it in a remarkable legal victory. The Court's majority opinion in *Smith v. Allwright* explicitly rejected the notion that the state's Democratic primary had a right to exclude black voters:

> The United States is a constitutional democracy. Its organic law grants to all citizens a right to participate in the choice of elected officials without restriction by any state because of race. This grant to the people of the opportunity for choice is not to be nullified by a state through casting its electoral process in a form which permits a private organization to practice racial discrimination in the election. Constitutional rights would be of little value if they could be thus indirectly denied.

Throughout the mid- to late 1940s, the NAACP obtained equally decisive victories against the white primary in other southern states, marking an important milestone in black Americans' struggle to obtain voting rights.

> Not only were more African Americans claiming their right to vote, but black men and women were exercising that right by electing militant politicians who would protect their interests. Civil rights leader and minister Adam Clayton Powell, Jr., was elected to the New York City Council in 1941 and to the U.S. House of Representatives in 1944, representing a new congressional district for Harlem, New York. On his

U.S. representative Adam Clayton Powell, Jr., (right) boards an Africa-bound flight with Ralph Bunche, United Nations undersecretary general (center), and Richard L. Jones, U.S. ambassador to Liberia (left), in 1960. Powell's militancy on civil rights issues raised the hackles of his fellow congressmen but made him wildly popular with his Harlem constituents.

first day in office, Powell engaged in a conversation with the speaker of the House, Representative Sam Rayburn. When Rayburn encouraged Powell to be moderate and soft-spoken and not to "throw those bombs," Powell replied, "Mr. Speaker, I've got a bomb in each hand and I'm going to throw them right away."

Powell was true to his word. He immediately became a one-man Jim Crow protest movement, barging into House facilities that were closed to African Americans. In 1946 he created what became known as the Powell Amendment when he attached a rider to a bill funding school-lunch programs that forbade the exclusion of African American children from the program. By the 1950s, he was attaching similar amendments to nearly every bill providing federal funds for education, thereby infuriating conservative southern congressmen. Powell's approach did not win him many friends on Capitol Hill, but his Harlem constituents loved it and reelected him 11 consecutive times, until a combination of scandal and illness lost him the Democratic nomination in 1970. Powell died in 1972; his funeral, attended by a multitude of mourners, was held in the Abyssinian Baptist Church in Harlem, where he had once preached.

Another great political leader, President Franklin Delano Roosevelt, died in April 1945. Black activists feared that the new administration might be hostile to civil rights, but Roosevelt's replacement and former vice president, Harry S. Truman, proved if anything more receptive to black concerns than his predecessor. In 1946, at the request of black activists, he

created the President's Committee on Civil Rights, which investigated racial and religious discrimination in housing, jobs, and justice.

The committee's report, *To Secure These Rights*, published in 1947, recommended specific action on behalf of various branches of government to rectify discrimination. The NAACP's Walter White was pleased both with Truman's cooperation and with the report itself, which he called "an almost perfect yardstick . . . by which can be measured the gap between what Americans say they believe and what they do."

The Truman administration was also intent on carrying out Roosevelt's vision of creating the United Nations, a worldwide organization that would promote international harmony and cooperation. Among the diplomats and luminaries from different countries

President Harry S. Truman— surrounded by African American activists, including Mary McLeod Bethune (third from left)—signs a proclamation that names each February 1 as Freedom Day. Truman, who proved surprisingly receptive to civil rights concerns, actively promoted nondiscrimination during his presidency.

who worked on drafting the United Nations Charter, one man stood out as a brilliant thinker, writer, diplomat, and administrator: Ralph Bunche. Formerly a prominent researcher for Gunnar Myrdal's *An American Dilemma*, Bunche worked for the Office of Strategic Services (the precursor of the Central Intelligence Agency) and the State Department during and after World War II. Bunche's academic background in international politics made him a natural choice for the American diplomatic team, and he was involved in the creation of the United Nations from 1942 onward.

Like many African Americans, Bunche was deeply concerned about the postwar fate of the European-controlled colonies in Africa and elsewhere. He believed that the colonial system was unjust and racist (one of its primary rationales being that nonwhites could not govern themselves), and he was certain that the world's colonies would eventually achieve independence, either through peaceful or violent means. Bunche felt that two major responsibilities of the United Nations should be to monitor colonial governments in order to curb injustices and to promote colonial independence through peaceful means.

European colonial powers and some American government officials opposed Bunche's stance and lobbied against any condemnation of colonialism. Their campaign was effective, and by the time of the United Nations founding conference in the spring of 1945, Bunche and the rest of the U.S. delegation had been instructed to take no stand on the issue of colonies.

Determined to see colonial issues addressed, Bunche quietly passed an unofficial draft of the U.S. position (written, in large part, by himself) to the Australian delegation. The Australians used the draft in creating their own proposal, which became the basis for the "Declaration Regarding Non-Self-Governing Territories," chapter 9 of the United Nations Charter.

Although Bunche, with characteristic modesty, wrote his wife that chapter 9 "is not as good as I would like it to be, but better than any of us expected it could get," an Australian diplomat described it as "the most far-reaching declaration on colonial policy in history."

Although chapter 9 did not mandate immediate independence for all colonies, it gave priority to the interests of colonized people and presented political independence as a desirable goal for all colonies. Bunche continually promoted colonial independence during his long and illustrious career (he won a Nobel Peace Prize in 1950, in addition to innumerable other honors) at the United Nations, a career that ended only with his death in 1971. Bunche's efforts paid off; according to his biographer Brian Urquhart in *Ralph*

Responding to an interviewer's questions, Ralph Bunche (right) discusses United Nations matters in a 1948 radio broadcast. Bunche, who helped draw up parts of the U.N. charter for trusteeships and non-self-governing territories, specialized in the promotion of peaceful decolonization.

Bunche: An American Life (1993), "decolonization was one of the comparatively rare success stories of the United Nations in the Cold War period."

Bunche was not the only black American to be prominently involved with the United Nations. Walter White, Mary McLeod Bethune, and W. E. B. Du Bois also formed part of the United Nations's founding conference, and White proved an able lobbyist when proposals came up before the United Nations General Assembly for votes. Being black was often an advantage in the world of international politics because, according to White, white diplomats sometimes showed a "racial arrogance toward the small countries because they were black and poor [that] was little different from that shown by the most intransigent southern politicians towards Negroes." Du Bois had long maintained that the fate of black Americans was linked to that of black Africans who suffered under the colonial system; now African Americans were increasingly in a position to better not only their own lot but that of their African fellows.

But for most African Americans, the best signal of black empowerment in the 1940s did not occur in an international conference or a somber courtroom. It took place on the grassy fields of a uniquely American sport.

Sports historians are unsure if black men played baseball before the Civil War (1861–65), but they know that black Union troops played the game at army camps, where they had watched their white colleagues practice the sport. The first professional black baseball team, organized in 1885, was made up of waiters from a New York State hotel; to avoid racism, the team billed itself as the Cuban Giants, and its members pretended to speak Spanish. By the 1890s, a few black men were playing for such important northern colleges as Amherst and Harvard, and major black stars, such as Paul Robeson—later famed as a great baritone—had emerged by 1918. But although some college squads were integrated, until almost the middle of the 20th century, no major league ball club boasted even a single black player.

A young man named Jack Roosevelt Robinson changed all that. Born in Cairo, Georgia, in 1919, Robinson attended the University of California at Los Angeles, where he became the school's first four-letter man; he excelled in basketball, football, baseball, and track. He led the basketball conference in scoring for two years in a row, won the national championship in the long jump, and, in 1940, was named an all-American halfback.

After Robinson entered the army as a draftee in 1941, he applied for Officer Candidate School (OCS). He was turned down because he was black. Characteristically, Robinson chose not to take the rejection meekly; he went to an influential friend and fellow draftee—World Heavyweight Champion Joe Louis—who used his influence to get Robinson admitted to OCS. Emerging a second lieutenant, Robinson spent the remainder of the war at bases in Kansas and Texas. Because he refused to accept second-class status—he would not sit in the back of the bus, for example, and he complained about the lack of seats for black servicemen in the base center—he was labeled a troublemaker and not permitted to go overseas. A later associate, Brooklyn Dodgers president Branch Rickey, talked of Robinson in these words:

> If he had done the things people are criticizing him for as a white . . . he would have been praised to the skies as a fighter, a holler guy, a real competitor, a ballplayer's ballplayer. But because he's black his aggressiveness is offensive to some.

Rickey, an extremely shrewd, innovative baseball executive, had long deplored baseball's "color line." He also deplored a losing team; these matched sentiments led him to work toward the seemingly impossible job of integrating baseball. Aware that the major leagues' refusal to admit African Americans deprived it of a huge number of potential stars, in the mid-1940s Rickey began sending his scouts to observe the Negro Leagues, a segregated arm of the sport, formed in 1920. Rickey's qualifications for the man he wanted were lofty: the first black man to play in the major leagues must be not only a superb athlete but one whose behavior outside the ballpark was equally impeccable. As biographer Richard Scott (in his 1987 book, *Jackie Robinson*), puts it, that man

> had to be strong enough to withstand the abuse and the pressures that would most certainly come his way. He could let nothing shake his self-confidence or his self-esteem, for to do so would surely affect his ability to concentrate on the game—and then the entire experiment of having a black play major league ball would fail. But if he were to succeed—then no one could question a black man's right to play in the major leagues.

The reports of Rickey's scouts zeroed in on one man: 26-year-old Jackie Robinson, then a shortstop for a Negro League team, the Kansas City Monarchs. Invited to come to New York to meet with Rickey, Robinson complied. He listened to the baseball executive describe the difficulties he would encounter if he agreed to join a white team, then, as he noted in his 1972 autobiography, *I Never Had It Made,* he asked, "Mr. Rickey, do you want a ballplayer who's afraid to fight back?"

"I want a player with guts enough not to fight back," said Rickey. He added that he wanted a man with the strength to ignore insults and even threats. Robinson realized that this meant he could never give in to his rage against bigotry, an extremely difficult condition for a man who had been fighting racism all his life. He thought long

and hard about Rickey's proposal. Then he responded. "If you want to take this gamble," he said quietly, "I will promise you there will be no incident."

Jackie Robinson (kneeling, first from left) appears in Venezuela with his American All-Star teammates in 1945, shortly before joining the Montreal Royals. Catcher Roy Campanella (standing, second from left) would follow Robinson to major league baseball stardom.

Robinson spent a year with the Dodgers' top farm club, the Montreal Royals. (A farm club is a minor league team where new recruits hone their skills for the major leagues.) In that year, he displayed the dazzling skill that would make him famous; he also suffered from a barrage of galling insults and jeers from violently prejudiced white baseball fans. His skill and his silence in the face of abuse eventually won him the affection and respect of his Montreal teammates. When the Royals finally won the league championship, the team displayed its feelings in full force, inspiring the Montreal fans to do the same. At the end

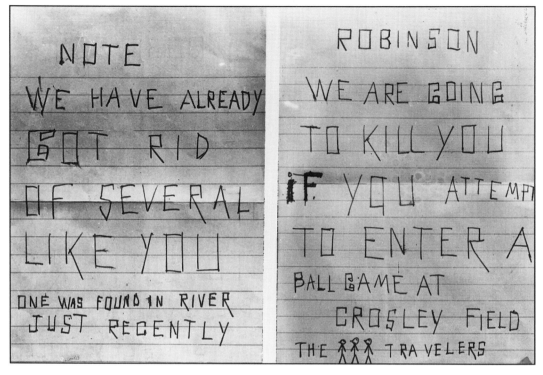

"We are going to kill you," begins this crude note of 1950. Racism in baseball hit a new low that year, as a spate of letters, all threatening violence if Jackie Robinson played at Cincinnati's Crosley Field, began appearing in baseball officials' offices. Robinson not only played in the Ohio stadium but won the game with a late-inning home run.

of the last, winning game, writes Scott, "the crowd poured into the field, chanting Robinson's name. Then they hoisted the young ballplayer above their shoulders and paraded him around the field. Sam Martin, a Montreal sportswriter, described the day's scene as 'probably the only day in history that a black man ran from a white mob with love instead of lynching on its mind.' "

By 1947, Robinson was playing for the Dodgers, helping his team win the National League pennant and getting named Rookie of the Year by *Sporting News* magazine. At first, although he inspired near worship from thousands of fans, black and white alike, he continued to be assaulted by the screaming insults of racists. During one particularly horrendous exhibit of racial venom, this one coming from members of the Philadelphia Phillies, Robinson recalled in his autobiography, he had a discussion with himself.

"What," Robinson thought, "did Mr. Rickey expect from me? I was, after all, a human being. What was I doing there turning the other cheek as though I weren't a man?" Then he considered his alternatives. "I could throw down my bat, stride over to that Phillies dugout, grab one of [them] . . . and smash his teeth in with my despised black fist." But Robinson took a deep breath and went on with the game, winning unanimous praise for his behavior from fans and sportswriters alike. "Jackie," noted the *New York Daily Mirror*, "with admirable restraint, ignored the guttersnipe language coming from the Phillies' dugout, thus stamping himself as the only gentleman among those involved in the incident."

Robinson's tumultuous first year with the Dodgers was only the beginning of a remarkable 10-year career with the team that resulted in his being elected in 1962 to the Baseball Hall of Fame. By 1949, his fortitude and refusal to react to abuse, along with his spectacular playing, had smoothed the way for other black men to follow his lead. Both Roy Campanella and Don Newcombe had joined the Dodgers when Rickey told Robinson he could drop the saintly posture. "Jackie, you're on your own now," Rickey said. "You can be yourself now." From then on, although Robinson never stooped to the gutter language of his tormentors, he stood up for himself, declining to ignore taunts. Talking to reporters about racist ballplayers in 1949, he said, "They'd better be rough on me this year, because I'm sure going to be rough on them."

Robinson's self-control was famous, but not all players could match his awesome composure in the face of insults; legendary pitcher Satchel Paige (hired by the major leagues in 1948), for example, ordinarily despised the beanball, but bragged of hitting one racist batter so hard that "he chased his hat and belt for half a block."

The defection of the top black talent to wealthier major league teams spelled the end of the Negro Leagues, which had been one of the most visible opportunities for black entrepreneurship. Nonetheless, the breaking of baseball's color barrier was a gigantic step in the quest for racial equality. The inclusion of African Americans in the major leagues demonstrated to many white Americans the absurdity of racist allegations that black Americans were mentally and physically incapable of competing at the highest levels. White fans would now look

Eyes on the ball, Jackie Robinson grimly ignores the racial heckling that dogged his every appearance in 1947. Despite torrents of abuse from the bleachers, the newly minted Dodger played superbly that year, hitting 12 home runs and helping his team snare the National League pennant.

to black baseball players as sports heroes, while African Americans had the satisfaction of seeing black talent recognized and rewarded.

Although very few people make the major leagues, and although baseball is not a major American industry, Robinson's breakthrough had enormous repercussions. The acknowledgment of African Americans' achievement on the ball field ultimately influenced the way they were seen and treated off it. As Paige told a group of retired black players in 1981: "They said we couldn't play ball. They said we had tails. But we showed 'em we're people just like anyone else."

As African Americans marched from 1931, the year that the infamous Scottsboro incident took place, to 1947, when Jackie Robinson trotted onto the ball field in a uniform once exclusively the white man's, the road began to grow wider, the passage smoother. At the beginning of this period, no black man who valued his life would approach a Deep South primary; after Thurgood Marshall talked to the Supreme Court in 1944, no law depriving that black man of his vote would stand. Indeed, black men and women had taken giant steps in all fields, from entertainment to education, from the Broadway theater to the theaters of war. Their achievements ranged from medical discoveries to medals of honor; they scored in the law courts and the diplomatic corps; they were named Academy Award winners and All-Americans. They still had many miles to cover—the great and bloody days of Selma, *Brown v. Board of Education*, the Freedom Rides, and the Black Panthers were still in the future—but by 1947, they had covered vast reaches, at last bringing them within hailing distance of their American birthright.

FURTHER READING

Aptheker, Herbert, ed. *A Documentary History of the Negro People in the United States, 1910–1932*. Secaucus, NJ: Citadel Press, 1973.

Bennett, Lerone, Jr. *Before the Mayflower: A History of Black America, 1619–1964*. New York: Penguin, 1988.

Carter, Dan T. *Scottsboro: A Tragedy of the American South*. Baton Rouge: Louisiana State University Press, 1979.

Franklin, John Hope. *From Slavery to Freedom: A History of Negro Americans*. New York: Knopf, 1987.

Hine, Darlene Clark, ed. *Black Women in America: An Historical Encyclopedia*. Brooklyn: Carlson Publishing, 1993.

Lincoln, C. Eric. *Race, Religion, and the Continuing American Dilemma*. New York: Hill & Wang, 1985.

McNeil, Genna Rae. *Groundwork: Charles Hamilton Houston and the Struggle for Civil Rights*. Philadelphia: University of Pennsylvania Press, 1983.

Myrdal, Gunnar. *An American Dilemma*. New York: Harper & Brothers, 1944.

Perrett, Geoffrey. *Days of Sadness, Years of Triumph: The American People, 1939–1945*. Madison: University of Wisconsin Press, 1985.

Peterson, R. *Only the Ball Was White: A History of Legendary Black Players and All-Black Professional Teams*. New York: McGraw Hill, 1984.

Scott, Richard. *Jackie Robinson*. New York: Chelsea House, 1987.

White, Walter F. *A Man Called White*. Salem, NH: Ayer, 1969.

INDEX

Abyssinian Baptist
Church, 22, 25, 136
African Americans
and education, 43–46,
49–57, 83
and labor unions, 20,
88–90, 92, 93, 98, 109,
131
and popular culture,
63–81, 140–47
violence against, 20, 21,
49, 102–7
and voting rights, 49,
133–36
women, 19–20, 22, 25,
27, 43–45, 57–61, 63,
101, 124–29, 131
and World War II,
97–129
Alexander, Raymond
Pace, 58
American Communist
party, 29–31, 79, 91–93,
95
*American Dilemma: The
Negro Problem and Mod-
ern Democracy, An,* 87–
88, 138
Anderson, Marian, 46, 47,
108
Armstrong, Louis, 67

Beavers, Louise, 68, 69, 70
Bell, Cool Papa, 74
Bethune, Mary McLeod,
43–46, 94, 111, 125, 140

Bethune-Cookman
College, 44
Binga, Jesse, 17–18
Binga State Bank, 17–18
Black Brain Trust, 45
Bogle, Donald, 65
Bolin, Jane Matilda, 60–61
Brotherhood of Sleeping
Car Porters (BSCP), 88–
90, 93
Bunche, Ralph, 86–87,
95, 138–40

Calloway, Cab, 68
Campanella, Roy, 145
Charleston, Oscar, 74
Congress of Racial Equal-
ity (CORE), 108
Count Basie, 68
Crutchfield, Jimmy, 74

Davis, Benjamin O., Sr.,
114, 117
Davis, Benjamin O., Jr.,
117
Daytona Normal and
Industrial Institute for
Negro Girls, 43–44
DePriest, Oscar, 40
Detroit race riot, 102–4,
105, 106, 107
Douglass, Frederick, 35, 39
Downey, Bill, 119–20
Drew, Charles Richard,
83–84

Du Bois, W. E. B., 81, 92,
95, 140

Ellington, Duke, 68
Executive Order 8802, 100

Fair Employment Prac-
tices Committee
(FEPC), 100
Fair Play Committee
(FPC), 70
Fard, W. D., 90, 91
Father Divine, 22, 23, 90
Father Divine Peace Mis-
sion, 22
Fauset, Crystal Bird, 61
Ford, James W., 30
Forrestal, James V., 124
Freeman, Susan Elizabeth,
126–27

Gaines, Lloyd, 55–56
Gibson, Joshua "Josh," 73-
75
Gray, Fred D., 42
Great Depression, 15–27,
35, 73, 79
Greenlee, Gus, 74
Grovey v. Townsend, 134

Harlem, New York City,
22, 23, 24, 135, 136
riot of 1935, 26–27, 105
riot of 1943, 105–6
Hastie, William, 45, 52–

53, 58
Holiday, Billie, 66–67
Hooks, Benjamin, 61
Horne, Frank, 45
Horne, Lena, 45
Housewives' League of
   Detroit, 25
Houston, Charles Hamil-
   ton, 51–52, 54–56, 57,
   58
Howard University, 52,
   53, 84, 86
Hughes, Langston, 92, 95

Interracial sexual rela-
   tions, 27, 29

"Jim Crow" laws, 50, 57,
   136
Johnson, John, 72
Johnson, Mordecai, 84

Ku Klux Klan, 100, 102,
   103

Lampkin, Daisy Adams,
   58, 59
Lee, Canada, 80
Louis, Joe, 75–76, 141
Lovett, Edward P., 58
Lynchings, 21, 38

McCoy, Cecil, 58
McDaniel, Hattie, 68, 69–
   70
McKay, Claude, 27
Marshall, Thurgood, 25,
   53–56, 57, 58, 134, 147
Micheaux, Oscar, 70–72
Miller, Dorie, 117, 118
Mitchell, Arthur W., 40
Mitchell, Clarence, 60
Mitchell, Juanita Jackson,

58, 60-61
Montgomery, Olen, 28
Muhammad, Elijah, 91
Murray v. Pearson, 54
Muse, Clarence, 70
Myrdal, Gunnar, 86–88,
   138

Nabrit, James M., 58
National Association for
   the Advancement of
   Colored People
   (NAACP), 20, 21, 24,
   25, 30, 38, 46, 49, 51,
   54, 55, 56, 57, 58, 59,
   60, 61, 69, 80, 83, 86,
   93, 104, 106, 133, 134,
   137
National Association of
   Colored Women
   (NACW), 58, 59
National Council of
   Negro Women
   (NCNW), 44, 59, 60
National Urban League,
   86, 124
National Youth Admini-
   stration (NYA), 36, 44,
   45, 46
Nation of Islam, 90, 95
Negro Baseball League,
   73, 146
Negro Industrial and
   Clerical League, 24
Negro Women's Franchise
   League, 59
Newcombe, Don, 145
99th Pursuit Squadron,
   117, 121
Norris, Clarence, 28, 31
Norris v. Alabama, 31

Owens, Jesse, 76–77
Oxley, Lawrence, 45

Paige, Satchel, 74, 145,
   147
Patterson, Haywood, 28
Patterson, William L., 30
Pearson, Conrad, 58
Pearson, Raymond, 54
Perry, Lincoln (Stepin
   Fetchit), 70
Peterson, Robert, 73, 75
Plessy v. Ferguson, 50, 57
Powell, Adam Clayton,
   Jr., 25, 106, 135–36
Powell, Ozie, 28
Powell v. Alabama, 30

Race riots, 21, 26–27,
   102–7
Randolph, A. Philip, 89,
   92, 93, 99, 101
Ransom, Leon A., 58
Rivers, Eunice, 41
Roberson, Willie, 28
Robeson, Paul, 92, 95, 140
Robinson, Bill "Bojan-
   gles," 64–66
Robinson, Jack Roosevelt
   "Jackie," 141–47
Roosevelt, Eleanor, 43,
   46, 47, 99, 112, 127
Roosevelt, Franklin
   Delano, 43

Scottsboro case, 27–31,
   92, 147
Segregation, 20, 21, 50–
   57, 61, 63, 64
   in baseball, 140–47
   in the military, 98, 111–
   29

"Separate but equal" doctrine, 50, 56, 57

Smith, Bessie, 67

Smith, Lonnie E., 134

Smith v. Allwright, 134

Spingarn Medal, 44, 46, 59, 80, 126

Staupers, Mabel, 126

Stepin Fetchit. *See* Perry, Lincoln

Supreme Court, U.S., 30, 31, 50, 51, 56, 57, 58, 61, 132–34, 147

Talbert, Mary Burnett, 58–59

332nd Fighter Group, 117, 121

Tuskegee Study of Untreated Syphilis in the Male Negro, 41–43

Tyson, James G., 58

United Nations, 137–40

Vann, Robert L., 39, 45

Washington, Booker T., 72

Weaver, Robert, 45

Webster, Milton, 99

White, Walter, 20–21, 38, 43, 46, 47, 57, 58, 59, 60, 69, 104, 122, 137, 140

Wilkins, Roy, 46, 127

World War I, 59, 83, 97, 111, 129

World War II, 83, 91, 93, 95, 97–129, 138

Wright, Louis T., 61

Wright, Richard, 78–81

DARLENE CLARK HINE, senior consulting editor of the MILESTONES IN BLACK AMERICAN HISTORY series, is the John A. Hannah Professor of American History at Michigan State University. She is the author of numerous books and articles on black women's history, as well as the editor of the two-volume *Black Women in America: An Historical Encyclopedia* (1993). Her most recent work is a collection of essays entitled *Hine Sight: Black Women and the Re-Construction of American History*.

CLAYBORNE CARSON, senior consulting editor of the MILESTONES IN BLACK AMERICAN HISTORY series, is a professor of history at Stanford University. His first book, *In Struggle: SNCC and the Black Awakening of the 1960s* (1981), won the Frederick Jackson Turner Prize of the Organization of American Historians. He is the director of the Martin Luther King, Jr., Papers Project, which will publish 12 volumes of King's writings.

PICTURE CREDITS